CONFLICT, CONTROVERSY AND CO-OPERATION

To the people of Greenisland Methodist Church
who accepted a difficult situation
'always … with grace and never hostility'

Norman W. Taggart

Conflict, Controversy and Co-operation

THE IRISH COUNCIL OF CHURCHES AND 'THE TROUBLES'
1968-1972

the columba press

First published in 2004 by
the columba press
55A Spruce Avenue, Stillorgan Industrial Park,
Blackrock, Co Dublin

Cover by Bill Bolger
Origination by The Columba Press
Printed in Ireland by ColourBooks Ltd, Dublin

ISBN 1 85607 438 2

Contents

Foreword

Norman Taggart was Secretary of the Irish Council of Churches at a critical moment in the history of Northern Ireland; the old order came under challenge and couldn't find an adequate response and a whole society collapsed into chaos and violence. Moreover, the situation could be plausibly – if simplistically – described as a religious conflict.

This book is the story of one person's creative response to a time of acute crisis. It is also the story of an ecumenical body, which comprised the major Protestant churches in Ireland, trying to act constructively in a context where many Protestants were deeply fearful and anxious, and believed that 'their' community was under attack. The pressure on the leadership of the Protestant churches was intense and this book charts some of their responses. The discussions around the time of internment are particularly illuminating.

The Second Vatican Council opened new ecumenical opportunities, but these new opportunities almost exactly coincided with a society descending into chaos and violence. Thus issues of ecumenism, community relations and responding to violence keep interacting. This book shows the Protestant churches and the Roman Catholic Church reaching out towards each other, often cautiously, hesitantly and fearfully, and particularly in the case of the Protestant churches looking over their shoulders for their members' responses – and always Paisley's aggressive and hectoring presence inhibiting action. It is a wonder so much was achieved, and some of the outstanding figures connected with the Council – and whose words and actions are recorded in these pages – deserve much praise: Principal James Haire, Dr Eric Gallagher, Archbishop George Simms. Norman Taggart's contribution also needs to be acknowledged. This book makes it clear that he wanted faster action and he was often frustrated (the fate of Secretaries) but he moved things on without losing the confidence of the key 'players'.

The story of the secret *ad hoc* Church Leaders Consultative Committee is fascinating and says much about the caution of some church leaders at the time. Thirty years on there has been a transformation in relationships between the churches but the period between 1968 and 1972 was when the first tentative steps were taken.

The Council and its Secretary played an honourable and creative role at a tumultuous time. I am grateful to Norman Taggart for telling the story.

David Stevens
General Secretary, Irish Council of Churches, 1992-2003
December 2003

Preface and Acknowledgements

I much appreciate the invitation from Dr David Stevens, the General Secretary of the Irish Council of Churches (the ICC), to write an account of the work of the ICC for the years 1968 to 1972 when I was part-time Organising Secretary. Dr Stevens and Joyce Williams, his Secretary, have given me access to minute books and other records at the Inter-Church Centre, Belfast. Dr Stevens also made helpful comments in the course of my writing and has contributed a generous foreword. Canon Robin Richey, my colleague in those years, has kindly supplemented my personal papers for the period.

Chapter 1 acknowledges that this is a personal account, coloured by my background and life experience, including the fact that during my years with the ICC I remained a minister active within the Methodist Church and was responsible for Greenisland Methodist church. For this reason, Methodism features more in the account than would have been the case had it been written by a full-time Secretary or a person from another church tradition. Chapter 2 focuses on the ICC's response to 'the Troubles', the crisis which began in Northern Ireland in 1968. The Troubles have continued to influence events ever since, causing immense suffering, deepening community divisions, necessitating radically different approaches to life but hopefully leading to the prospect of a better future for all. Chapter 3 discusses new relationships between the Council and the Roman Catholic Church. Chapters 2 and 3 are central to the work, each containing important new material. An indication of political and community developments is included, since they provided the inescapable backdrop to daily life at that time. In this connection account is taken of recent research and revelations which throw light on events and relationships between 1968 and 1972. Chapter 4 assesses 'success' and 'failure' in the ICC at the time, and briefly considers present day challenges. Other areas of activity within the ICC included youth work, Christian Aid and world development, ecumenical education, and local and wider ecumenical contacts. These are commented upon as they related to the main concerns taken up in chapters 2 and 3.

On occasions I draw attention to statements I made through sermons and addresses, which were often reported in the media. Some people might question the appropriateness of these in a book not on my own ministry but on the ICC. The statements were however part of my response to the tasks given me by the Council, which included advocating and interpreting ecumenism. They also reflect my conviction at the time that there had to be contact and integrity between my work for the ICC and as minister of Greenisland Methodist church. The statements are part of one story, providing personal comment on issues with which the Council was concerned.

In addition to Dr Stevens and Canon Richey, a number of other people have helped in the preparation of this book. They include Dr Robert Brown, Barry Deane (now a Lay Canon) and Dr David Poole, who served with me on the ICC and its Executive; Geoffrey Corry, Dr Gordon Gray, Cecil Hyland, John Knox and Foster Murphy, who were then active on the youth scene; Canon Robert M. C. Jeffery, then on the staff of the British Council of Churches; Margaret Boden and Dr David Lapsley, whom I consulted on Christian Aid at that time; Cardinal Cahal Daly, Michael Hurley and Bishop Patrick Walsh, who shared with me on Roman Catholic attitudes and ecumenical involvement during the period; and Dr Ian Ellis, a former President of the ICC and author of *Vision and Reality*, a survey of twentieth century Irish inter-church relations. Dr Dennis Cooke, Principal of Edgehill Theological College, is currently engaged on a biography of Dr Eric Gallagher to be published by the Epworth press in the autumn 2004. Dr Gallagher also features prominently in these pages. In this connection Dr Cooke gave me access to private papers which added to my understanding of Dr Gallagher's involvement in events between 1968 and 1972. I gladly acknowledge this. Hopefully our conversations have benefitted both of us.

Norman Taggart
Lower Ballinderry

Abbreviations

BCC	British Council of Churches
CA	Christian Aid
CCB	Belfast Council of Churches ('CCB' to distinguish the Belfast Council of Churches from 'BCC' for the British Council of Churches)
CEC	Conference of European Churches
C of I	Church of Ireland
CSI	Church of South India
DCC	Dublin Council of Churches
DUP	Democratic Unionist Party
EA	Evangelical Alliance
EYCE	Ecumenical Youth Council of Europe
ICC	Irish Council of Churches
ICYA	Irish Christian Youth Assembly
IICM	Irish Inter-Church Meeting
IRA	Irish Republican Army
ISE	Irish School of Ecumenics
MCI	Methodist Church in Ireland
MMS	Methodist Missionary Society
NICRA	Northern Ireland Civil Rights Association
NILP	Northern Ireland Labour Party
NIO	Northern Ireland Office
NIVCOAD	Northern Ireland Voluntary Committee on Overseas Aid and Development
PACE	Protestant and Catholic Encounter
PCI	Presbyterian Church in Ireland
RCC	Roman Catholic Church
RUC	Royal Ulster Constabulary
SDLP	Social Democratic and Labour Party
SODEPAX	Joint Committee on Society, Development and Peace
UCCI	United Council of Christian Churches and Religious Communions in Ireland
UDA	Ulster Defence Association
UUP	Ulster Unionist Party
UVF	Ulster Volunteer Force
WCC	World Council of Churches
WPCU	Week of Prayer for Christian Unity
WWDP	Women's World Day of Prayer
YCIC	Youth Committee of Irish Churches

CHAPTER ONE

A Personal Perspective

This is a personal perspective on the role and influence of the Irish Council of Churches between 1968 and 1972, the early years of 'the Troubles' as we euphemistically call them. The deteriorating situation within the community formed the continuing backdrop to everyday life and prompted many of the responses and initiatives taken by the ICC. Both words – *personal* and *perspective* – are important. Other people would have described the work of the ICC differently. Having had a part-time position in the ICC at the time, I write as an 'insider' whose outlook has been influenced by my upbringing and education mainly in Belfast and by periods of ministry in Sandy Row, Belfast (1961-2), India (1962-6), Sligo (1966-8), Greenisland (1968-72), London (1972-9), the Belfast Central Mission (1979-87), Cavehill (1987-9), Sri Lanka (1990-4) and Coleraine and Ballymoney (from 1994 until my retirement in 2001). The reasons for writing include the invitation from the Secretary of the ICC, Dr David Stevens; the fact that earlier accounts of the ICC in the period have tended to be rather sketchy, often being part of wider studies; the number of people still alive who were involved then in the ICC is decreasing gradually; as the Organising Secretary, I possess personal records and memories; and perhaps most tellingly, my retirement has provided time and opportunity to put pen to paper.

My childhood was spent in Woodvale, a working class district in Belfast. Our home was not conventional from a political point of view, being unionist with only a small 'u'. We favoured Labour or socialist politics more than the flag-waving form of unionism which prevailed. Unionist myths that somehow the Protestant working class was 'the people', superior to the Roman Catholic working class in every way, whether or not either side had jobs, cut little ice with us. At home, anger was sometimes expressed at the injustices from which the poor – Protestants as well as Catholics – suffered. Such stances made us aware that in a sense we were part of a minority within the Protestant majority in Northern Ireland. Socially and politically we therefore had at least a small degree of fellow feeling with the much larger Catholic minority, sharing with them a sense of powerlessness to influence events. The short-term rise in the fortunes of the Northern Ireland Labour Party (NILP) from the late 1950s heartened us, holding out hope of better days to come. Religiously we were Methodists, another minority grouping. Methodism sharpened our social and community conscience, softened our attitudes towards Catholics in a society scarred by sectarianism, and arising from its Arminianism and 'the optimism of grace'[1] helped to keep us fundamentally hopeful despite the odds against us. Later, in the 1980s, I was to use three words to describe Irish Methodism – 'slender', 'struggling' and 'fruitful'[2] – to draw attention to the fact that, though small, Methodism in Ireland has at best responded positively to the challenge of being a religious minority and has borne fruit.

Thirty years after an anti-UDA (Ulster Defence Association) statement made by me in June 1972,[3] I learnt of a conversation between my father and one of my brothers. By then the Troubles had taken their toll on our father, shaking his confidence, hardening his attitudes and making him more conservative. The UDA was already strong around Woodvale in 1972, where our parents still lived, and my father had apparently been 'very upset' by the statement, though he never discussed it with me. Perhaps he felt vulnerable in the circumstances. Where had I got 'that stuff', he had asked. My brother, never one to flinch from pressing a point, simply replied 'from you'.

I have had two main concerns throughout my life, mission and unity. Not one for labels, I have none the less always considered myself an evangelical and an ecumenist. This has not been a common combination among evangelicals in Northern Ireland due to the widespread fear and mistrust of Roman Catholic teaching, practice and motivation, coupled with an assumption that vital Reformation principles might somehow be compromised through association with Catholics. The phrase 'Romeward trend' was widely used among those opposed to the ecumenical movement in the 1960s and 70s, referring to a likely 'sell-out to Rome' by so-called 'ecumenical churches'.

After studying at Queen's University and Edgehill College, where Methodist ministers (and nowadays lay people of varying traditions) are trained, I was sent with Margaret, my wife, to Selly Oak Colleges, Birmingham, for one year's further training for service overseas. This was followed by a year's exposure to practical ministry in Sandy Row, Belfast, a 'missionary' situation as demanding and challenging as any we were later to encounter elsewhere in the world. Many people in Sandy Row were unchurched. Some were 'political Protestants', hostile or indifferent to the Christian faith, pro-British and anti-Catholic. Others, however, were deeply committed Christians, exerting a lasting and wholesome influence upon us. During this year in Belfast we occasionally visited Anthony and Miriam Hanson who had worked for over a decade within the united Church of South India (CSI), to be given an informal introduction to life in India and the Telugu language. Anthony Hanson had been appointed canon theologian at St Anne's Church of Ireland Cathedral, Belfast, to encourage C of I clergy to undertake further studies. The appointment was not, however, universally welcomed within the the C of I since some people – bishops included – were rather cool towards the CSI.

I was ordained and served in the Medak diocese of the CSI, a church formed in 1947 which brought together mainly Anglicans, Congregationalists, Methodists and Presbyterians. The CSI recognised and sought to give practical expression to the link between mission and unity. In our part of rural India, Andhra Pradesh, a predominantly Hindu society in which there was an influential and sizeable Muslim minority, we learnt to respect and work with people of other faiths. Despite long-standing restrictions concerning conversion where we first served, a leprosy hospital in and around which there was a 'no proselytism' rule, we found it possible to relate to people in ways relevant to their needs. India influenced us profoundly, opening us up to unfamiliar, richly textured cultures, and helping us to grow as people. We also matured through a painful experience of uncertainty, illness and family separation. We had gone to India with a one-year-old daughter. Our second child, a son, was born there. Due to his serious illness when under two years of age, Margaret and the children were forced to return suddenly to Ireland, leaving me behind. Six months later I too returned to Ireland after completing the Indian church year, and was appointed to Sligo in February 1966, a predominantly Roman Catholic community now more open to cross-community initiatives following the Second Vatican Council.

Our time in India had coincided with the holding of the Vatican Council between 1962 and 1965. Life in a remote part of rural India – an area in which most people were illiterate, communication with the outside world was rudimentary, and Christians were a tiny minority with the nearest Catholic priest several miles away – meant that the excitement and significance of the Second Vatican Council had passed us by. To live thereafter for a couple of years in Sligo was ideal, enabling us to be together again as a family, helping us to catch up with changes in the mood and spirit of Roman Catholicism, and facilitating a stimulating and fulfilling short period of cross-community ministry at a time of continuing uncertainty, while the possibility of returning to India was explored.

I was appointed part-time Secretary of the Irish Council of Churches (ICC) in 1968 when hopes of returning to India were finally frustrated. The Council appointment was initially for three years, subject to satisfactory decisions being taken at the Methodist Conference in June, and was to become effective from the late summer. The Conference duly obliged, transferring me from Sligo to Greenisland on the county Antrim side of Belfast Lough, a location close to Belfast and convenient to the access routes to Dublin, the two centres for most ICC activities. From a Methodist point of view, Greenisland is on the Carrickfergus Circuit with four churches, Carrickfergus, Greenisland, Islandmagee and Whitehead. Though I was to be responsible for the church at Greenisland, I would also be required to take occasional services in each of the other churches. Few people at the Methodist Conference would have realised that part of the reason for my transfer was to enable me to take up an appointment with the ICC. It was not that the ecumenical element in the transfer was deliberately played down. Reference to my ICC appointment had been made in the ICC report received at Conference, but as far as I am aware no reference was made to it within Conference discussions or later in the published minutes of Conference. This indeed was the pattern throughout my period with the ICC, as it was for other Methodists involved with the Council including Dr Gallagher, the ICC Chairman from 1967 to 1969. It was probably more a case of low-profile ecumenism than ecumenism by stealth, a strategy encouraged by circumstances. I now, however, also see it as an indication that though Methodism has been 'up front' about its membership of the ICC, ecumenical involvement has somehow tended not to be regarded as being within the mainstream of the church's life and witness. Ecumenism in the 1960s, especially in the North, was viewed as a minority interest – far down the list of priorities – or as an ecclesiastical hot potato, to be handled, if at all, with extreme caution and as little publicity as possible.

I discovered on arrival at Greenisland that only a handful of local people were aware of my coming ICC responsibilities. In a way this low-key approach was understandable, given the cool, even hostile ecumenical climate. In retrospect, however, one wonders about the wisdom and fairness of such an arrangement. Have ecumenical activists been made to pay too high a price for their involvement? Could not more have been done to affirm and support them? Most local people in Greenisland simply regarded me as their new minister, whom they expected to be with them full-time. As already noted, nothing in the minutes of Conference indicated that I would have other commitments. Interestingly, the Presbyterian Church had handled matters quite differently some years earlier, when Carlisle Patterson's part-time secretaryship of the United Council of Churches and Religious Communions in Ireland (UCCI) – while still an active minister within the PCI – was officially endorsed and recognised within Presbyterianism. I was placed in an awkward position. Would the people in Greenisland understand my position when they came to realise, as inevitably they would, that I had other commitments? Would I be able to keep on top of things locally, providing a level of pastoral care and leadership which the people had a right to expect? Had the Greenisland congregation learnt of a comment in a Sligo newspaper in July 1968,[4] that my transfer from Sligo was 'only incidental' to my taking up an appointment with the ICC, my endeavour to win people's confidence in Greenisland might well have been lost at the outset.

Could I at the same time establish and maintain good relations within the ICC? Could I measure up to their expectations of me? Only time would tell. I was conscious that with few exceptions I was not well known to many people in ICC circles. I did not come from one of the two main member churches (the Church of Ireland and the Presbyterian Church), and I was still in the early years of my ministry and had been overseas. I was fortunate though in that Dr Eric Gallagher (he was to receive an honorary doctorate in 1971) – who did know me – was the current Chairman of the ICC as well as being President of the Methodist Church in 1967-8, and I could only assume that he and others such as Harold Sloan, the Secretary of the Methodist Conference, had sufficient confidence in me to commend me to other Council members. Principal James Haire, who was to succeed Dr Gallagher as Chairman of the ICC, was acquainted with me through my training for ministry in the late 1950s in shared classes at Edgehill College and the Presbyterian Assembly's (later Union) College where he was now Principal. Robert Brown (the Convener of the Presbyterian Inter-Church Relations Committee) and Gordon Gray (the Presbyterian Youth Secretary) had been fellow ministerial students with me and were now involved in the ICC, as was Canon Eric Elliott (C of I) who had taught me 'RE' at 'Inst' (the Royal Belfast Academical Institution).

Whatever uncertainties may have weighed on our minds, we were soon left in no doubt as to the goodwill which awaited us as a family in Greenisland. My two ministerial colleagues on the Methodist Circuit, including Samuel Ferguson my Superintendent minister, were warm and welcoming. Our new home on Station Road was close to the Methodist church which faced the Church of Ireland building across the road. The two churches shared one Boys' Brigade company and on occasions co-operated in other ways. Harden Johnston, the rector, was a close and friendly neighbour. A housing estate, with Protestant and Catholic residents, was within sight. The local RC chapel stood a little distance away, just off the Station Road. The Presbyterian church was on the Upper Road, towards Carrickfergus. Soon after our arrival, Margaret was invited to a coffee morning to meet some of the neighbours in the Attwood home. The Attwoods were Catholics, with their son Alex a schoolboy in those days. He was later to become a leading figure in the Social Democratic and Labour Party (SDLP), a merger of several nationalist political groups in 1970. That same year – one in which the battle lines were being drawn between pro- and anti-reform parties and politicians in Northern Ireland – also saw the emergence of the moderate Alliance Party, with which some of our Greenisland Methodists were to associate. Local community relations appeared good in 1968. Margaret and I eagerly anticipated the fresh challenges we have always found in the appointments in which the itinerant system of ministry in the Methodist Church has placed us.

In 1967-8 the member churches of the ICC were the Church of Ireland, the Congregational Union, the Methodist Church, the Moravian Church, the Non-Subscribing Presbyterian Church, the Presbyterian Church, the Religious Society of Friends and the Salvation Army. Within a year the Congregational Union withdrew from the Council, apparently not for any theological reason or because of disagreement. Towards the end of my period the Lutheran Church came into membership, restoring the number of member churches to eight. The ICC was also associated with the Youth Committee of the Irish Churches (YCIC), the Churches' Industrial Council, Christian Aid (the development agency of forty churches in Britain and Ireland), and local Councils of Churches (especially in Belfast and Dublin). Its officers were Dr Gallagher, Chairman; Principal James Haire, Vice-Chairman; Canon Robin Richey, Secretary; and John Radcliffe, Honorary Treasurer. With my appointment as Organising Secretary, Robin Richey became Assistant and Records' Secretary. In this capacity he gave me invaluable support and encouragement over the next four years, servicing committees, writing the Council and Executive minutes (on which I have drawn for this work), relieving me of aspects of administration, and undertaking other work for the Council, especially as it related to the Republic.

The ICC summarised my tasks as advocating and interpreting ecumenism; making contact with local churches and with local Councils of Churches; monitoring the new relationships, official and unofficial, between the Irish churches including the Roman Catholic Church; working for increased co-operation between the departments of member churches; and through liaison with the British Council of Churches, making progress in these areas. Although no direct reference was made to the churches' role in society, this was never far from mind and it quickly became my most daunting, demanding and controversial area of activity. The tasks as listed were described as my 'primary duty'. What else was in mind, one wonders? It was a tall order for one of two part-time staff persons – the other being Robin Richey – each working from home on a part-time basis, in a body which in view of the anticipated increase in activity asked its member churches to raise their combined giving to £1080 per year. The initial payment for the two members of staff came to a total of £350 per annum, plus expenses. After a few years, I was in addition provided with a dictating machine and local part-time secretarial help, and my term as Organising Secretary was extended to 1972.

In retrospect, how did the shared appointment with the ICC work out from Greenisland's point of view? Involvement with the ICC undoubtedly meant that I was unavailable locally at times, and I always felt apprehensive when my ecumenical activity involved me in public controversy and criticism. As early as February 1969 an article by me in the Methodist *Irish Christian Advocate*, entitled 'The unity that really matters', was given as one of two reasons why a regular reader of the paper for over thirty years cancelled his order. 'I think it would have been a good day for Irish Methodism had Mr Taggart stayed with the Church of South India', he wrote in a letter to the editor.[5] My ministry in Greenisland was enriched by wider contacts through the ICC, and local people were remarkably understanding and supportive of my work with the Council. Methodist Circuit minutes record many positive developments in Greenisland between 1968 and 1972. These included a successful stewardship campaign, forming a team to undertake practical work on the premises, membership classes leading to the reception of new church members of varied ages, experimental services, youth and children's programmes, and work among women reported as flourishing. Local Methodists became involved in cross-community initiatives. For example, the peace movement Women Together became active in Greenisland, with the local branch described as one of the largest in the country.

Our family increased by two during the time, with the arrival for adoption of an Indo Mauritian baby boy early in 1969 and a Jamaican baby girl a year later. My final Circuit Quarterly meeting was held in Greenisland in early June 1972, when tributes were paid to my ministry. In response I referred to the fact that I 'had always been received with grace and never hostility' in the churches of the Circuit.[6] Later in the month, at a congregational event to say farewell to us as a family, the presence of Archbishop George Simms, by then the ICC Chairman, and Dr Gallagher – both representing the wider church and my ICC involvement – was much appreciated.

CHAPTER 2

The ICC and the Northern Ireland Crisis

Setting the Scene

My years as Organising Secretary of the ICC coincided with the first four years of the Troubles, the crisis in Northern Ireland which began in 1968 and continued through various phases into the twenty-first century. Created in conflict, with a large and reluctant Catholic minority, Northern Ireland experienced difficult periods from the outset but on a much lesser scale than in the Troubles. Notable were the riots following Orange parades in 1935, which left eleven people dead; and the IRA's border-campaign of 1956-1962, which failed to provoke significant numbers of Protestants and Roman Catholics into becoming involved. Following student unrest around the world and international calls for civil rights in the 1960s, the mainly nationalist Catholic minority in Northern Ireland began to focus less on issues related to the border between the two parts of Ireland, and more on its grievances as a minority within the North. Led by a new generation of university trained professionals and students, the minority's call for civil rights and reforms within Northern Ireland began to attract wider interest and sympathy within and beyond the Province. The Northern Ireland Civil Rights Association (NICRA) was established in January 1967, with the task of spearheading a civil rights campaign. These developments greatly increased feelings of uncertainty and insecurity within the mainly unionist Protestant majority, which feared that changes would lead to a lessening of the links with Britain and ultimately to the formation of an independent, predominantly Roman Catholic thirty-two county Ireland in which Protestants would suffer as a religious minority. Protestant fear of RC domination has a long history in Ireland, expressed for example in the 'Home rule is Rome rule' slogan and encouraged by 'church and state' controversies following partition. Some in the Northern majority were convinced that the demand for reforms was merely a subterfuge, not genuinely motivated by concern for human rights but originating with sinister, left-wing, republican forces, North and South, the main objective of which was to overthrow the Northern Ireland state. Significantly, the thirteen-person committee initially chosen to run NICRA included two representatives from Wolfe Tone Societies (radical republican discussion groups) and a member of the IRA. At another level, the rise in support for the NILP, coupled with the presence at Westminster of Labour Prime Minister Harold Wilson who was viewed as unsympathetic to the unionist government, was also deeply unsettling for many within the Northern Ireland majority. Against this background, Captain Terence O'Neill, the Northern Ireland Prime Minister since 1963, recognised the need for reform and sought to pursue a reformist course, promoting cross-border economic links and attempting to accommodate an increasingly educated Catholic minority within Northern Ireland.

What substance was there in Protestant fears of what they preceived as a hidden hostile agenda within the Catholic minority, and the claims from within the Catholic minority that they were the victims of neglect, systematic discrimination, unfair treatment and oppression? Opinion was divided throughout society, within and between the churches and among politicians. Many within the majority community perceived the Catholic minority *per se* as enemies of the state, deliberately pursuing an abstentionist policy which posed a threat to the existence of Northern Ireland and its continuance within the United Kingdom. Such thinking served to explain, and was used in an attempt to justify, discrimination by the majority against the minority. Catholics, for their part, felt that the Protestant/unionist majority had deliberately frozen them out of participation within the life of Northern Ireland since its creation, excluding them from positions of influence and power. After all, Lord Craigavon, the first N. I. Prime Minister, had himself famously referred to Northern Ireland in 1934 as 'a Protestant Parliament and a Protestant State'. On the other hand, de Valera, head of the Irish government, had spoken of Ireland on St Patrick's Day the following year as 'a Catholic nation'.

The basic aims of NICRA were 'one man, one vote' in local elections rather than a property qualification, which though equally binding on Protestants and Catholics affected Catholics disproportionately; the re-drawing of electoral boundaries by an independent commission; legislation against discrimination by local authorities and machinery to remedy local government grievances; a compulsory and fair points system in the allocation of public housing; the repeal of the Special Powers Act; and the disbanding of the Ulster Special Constabulary (widely known as the 'B' Specials), an exclusively Protestant part-time police force. Intentionally non-sectarian, with both socialist republicans and 'for the most part, people with far less radical vews'[1] within its membership, the civil rights campaign became increasingly associated in Protestant eyes with republicanism. Brinkmanship, including high profile protest marches over government 'law and order' restrictions, became major factors in this perception.

As an all-Ireland religious body with no political affiliations, the ICC's stand in favour of human rights, including the need for reforms in the North, became clear and consistent. With tensions increasing from the mid 60s onwards, the Council was concerned to speak and act constructively through its Executive Committee and biannual meetings. The fact that it was the official ecumenical instrument of member churches which also existed on an all-Ireland basis, gave an edge to its discussions and made it difficult for it to view matters simply from a narrow Northern Protestant perspective. Northern rather than all-Ireland concerns did, however, tend to dominate the ICC's agenda, as indeed they did the agendas of all 'non-Catholic' churches whether or not they were members of the ICC. A partial exception was the Church of Ireland, for historical and traditional reasons. To an extent this focus on the North was inevitable, given the serious turn of events within that part of the island and the fact that the majority of Protestant church members lived either within Northern Ireland or along the troubled border areas. The Dublin Council of Churches (DCC), founded in 1964, helped to redress this imbalance. As was normally the case with local Councils of Churches, it was composed of congregational rather than denominational units, each member congregation in the Dublin area being represented by its clergy and two lay representatives. With the ICC focusing mainly on the North, especially during the Troubles, the DCC tended to fulfil the functions of a national Council in the South as circumstances required, though it was sensitive to the fact that it was not truly representative of the Republic as a whole. One example was when the DCC, in consultation with the ICC, examined with the Southern authorities whether there was a need for a residential home for young Protestant offenders in the Republic.

Topics considered by the ICC between 1966 and the start of my appointment in 1968 included the effects of the fiftieth commemoration of the 1916 'Easter Rising' in Dublin, with Ian Paisley attempting to whip up fears of a mass incursion by republicans from the South; dialogue on ecumenism with the Orange and Black Institutions; the cancellation, following protests and demonstrations, of an invitation to the Anglican Bishop of Ripon, Dr J. R. H. Moorman, to preach in St Anne's Cathedral, Belfast (he was chair of the international Joint Anglican/Roman Catholic Commission); and the new year message in 1968 by the two Archbishops of Armagh (Catholic and C of I) and the Methodist President and Presbyterian Moderator, the first of its kind. Two quotations in connection with the Bishop of Ripon affair give a flavour of discussions within the Council. 'Civil and religious liberty can never be equated with blatant attempts to suppress free speech', and:

> A continuation of these agitations, demonstrations and pressures to which Belfast is being ... subjected in the name of religion can only drive increasing numbers into cynicism and open hostility to organised religion of any kind.[2]

In time the seriously damaging effects of bitter religious controversies were to become ever more apparent to people – Christians and others – in Ireland and across the world.

July to December 1968

Five of those who represented their churches on the ICC also attended the fourth assembly of the World Council of Churches (WCC) held at Uppsala, Sweden, from 4 to 20 July 1968. With the scriptural theme 'Behold, I make all things new' (Revelation 21:5), this gathering was the WCC's most activist and politically oriented assembly. As the ICC sought to respond to Uppsala, special note was taken of a section in the assembly report which was seen to speak directly to the rapidly deteriorating situation within Northern Ireland. Although torn by 'diversities and tensions' and not yet knowing how to live together, the report declared, all people had in some senses already become 'neighbours to one another'. Christ wanted his worldwide church 'to foreshadow a renewed human community', with his followers manifesting their unity by 'entering into full fellowship with those of other races, classes, age, religious and political convictions', where they lived.

A civil rights march in Derry on 5 October 1968 brought matters to a head within Northern Ireland, and provided an urgent local context in which the words from Uppsala demanded to be interpreted and applied. More than any other single event, the march and the public reaction to it can be said to have launched the Troubles. Television pictures flashed around the world showing the police batoning marchers, including members of parliament, without 'justification or excuse' according to the Cameron Commission which reported the following September. Local hospitals reported treating seventy-seven civilian casualties, mainly with bruises and lacerations to the head. Among them was Gerry Fitt who had been an MP at Westminster for a Belfast constituency since 1966. 'The perception rapidly developed', wrote two commentators, that 'something was rotten in the state of Northern Ireland', adding that unionists, long used to stability and easy political victories, found it difficult 'to defend the peculiarities of their system' and 'to deal with a real crisis'. A complicating and contributory factor in the day's disorder and violence was the failure of those organising the march to take account of 'the confused cross-currents of student radicalism'.[3]

A special meeting of the Belfast Council of Churches (CCB) was convened on 14 October to discuss this serious turn of events and to consider what action might be taken.The meeting was chaired by Achdeacon John Mercer, and attended by the Chairman of the ICC and other ICC members including myself. Since church leaders and others had already issued statements, it was decided not to make another statement but instead to send four people to talk to politicians and to report back the following week. A further meeting of the CCB was held on 21 October when Professor James Boyd of the PCI reported on interviews in which he and the CCB's officers (John Mercer and David Turtle, the latter the Methodist chaplain at Queen's University) had met in turn with two Nationalist poiticians (Eddie McAteer and Austin Currie) and two Unionist politicians (the Prime Minister, Captain Terence O'Neill, and Brian Faulkner). A statement was released to the press by the CCB, asking for extremism and unfair discrimination to be 'utterly outlawed', grievances to be examined, and progressive policies to be pursued for example on electoral methods at local elections, the provision and allocation of houses and the creation of job opportunities. At this meeting with the Prime Minister and Faulkner, or possibly at another on 29 October – there is a discrepancy over dates – Faulkner took a much less liberal line than he was later to advocate in public, in which he resisted the introduction of 'one man one vote' in local elections and argued that there was nothing in Northern Ireland of which Unionists 'needed to be ashamed'.[4]

At an ICC Executive Committee meeting, also on 21 October, serious concern was expressed about the violence which had erupted during and after the civil rights march in Derry. Against this background it was suggested that there should be consultation with representatives of the Roman Catholic Church to find out if the churches together could act in the interests of community relations. Carlisle Patterson said it was important for the Council to open regular lines of communication with Catholic leaders to enable the churches to respond quickly to community crises. Noel Mackey – C of I and involved in the Churches' Industrial Council (formed in 1959 as the first body in Ireland through which Protestants and Catholics sought to work together in the area of industry and employment) – stressed the need for the facts relating to election procedures and the allocation of houses to be established. It was agreed that the ICC should go into closed session at its Council meeting in Belfast on 7 November, to discuss community relations and the possibility of an approach to the Roman Catholic hierarchy.

On 4 November Terence O'Neill, with William Craig and Brian Faulkner, met the British Prime Minister, Harold Wilson, in London. The Prime Minister warned that reforms had to be introduced by the N. I. government. If not, the British government might consider 'the complete liquidation of all financial agreements with Northern Ireland'.[5] Wilson publicly repeated the pledge given in 1949 in the wake of the Republic of Ireland Act, that there would be no transfer of N. I. to the Republic without the consent of the N. I. parliament. Such statements had a destabilising effect, disturbing rather than reassuring the majority.

Discussions in the closed session of the ICC in Belfast led to a public statement and course of action agreed without dissent. It called for restraint on the streets and for reforms, and authorised an approach to the Catholic hierarchy. The statement was publicly released and received wide coverage in the media. Key phrases included these:

> We support appeals for urgent investigation and remedy of authentic grievances ... Churches have a serious obligation to challenge more of (their) members to participate actively in civic and political life ... in the interests of the whole community ... Further demonstrations will impede progress in reform; but the government and local authorities must more urgently consider the need for reforms, especially in work opportunities, allocation of housing and local franchise ... We hope our Roman Catholic and other fellow-countrymen will (see how) they can alleviate the effects of those of their policies which tend to divide the community ... We direct our Executive Committee to consult with responsible Church leaders on practical steps to advance the work of reconciliation...

The shift from 'community relations', as in the Executive resolution in October, to 'reconciliation' and the direct reference to the need for 'practical steps', indicated some progress in thought and a recognition of the need to match words with action. The direct reference to Catholics, in connection with all those whose policies tended to divide the community, was a signal and appeal that both sides needed to take fears and perceptions seriously, and to engage in serious thinking about issues which tended to divide. Though not publicly stated, matters discussed included the Catholic attitude towards Northern Ireland, ab-

stentionist politics, mixed marriages, cultural celebrations including marches, and separate education.

Two days later, after consultation with Belfast-based members of the ICC Executive, it was agreed that representatives of
the ICC should take steps to facilitate consultation between the
leaders of the larger ICC member churches, RC leaders and the
Council. This way of taking things forward was felt to be best in
the circumstances, recognising that the churches had a higher
profile than the ICC (their ecumenical instrument), and that sensitivities within the churches and the Council itself required that
the ICC did not appear to 'take the lead' or to act independently
of its member churches. This discreet approach was approved
by the ICC Executive on 22 November. At this meeting Noel
Mackey and Carlisle Patterson pressed 'the need to set up a permanent consultative body' with Roman Catholics 'to consider
social problems', in the belief that 'occasional consultations in
times of crisis' would simply not be adequate. Members of the
ICC Executive were also appointed at the meeting of the
Executive on 22 November to consult with Protestant church
leaders later the same day on how and when to approach the RC
leaders. Patterson was to take up a position with the Conference
of British Missionary Societies in London in 1970, and became
Head of the Overseas Aid Department of Christian Aid in 1976.
His departure was a serious loss to the developing ecumenical
scene within Ireland.

Coincidentally 22 November was also the day on which the
N. I. government issued a five-point package of reform, later admitted by the N. I. Prime Minister to be 'small' and 'timid'. The
planned reforms could have gone some way towards easing the
grievances of Catholics had they been able to be presented as the
granting of acknowledged rights rather than a grudging response to mounting pressures. Their announcement, however,
caused dissension within the Stormont cabinet, and greatly
heightened feelings of insecurity within an ill-prepared majority
community. On 9 December 1968 Terence O'Neill felt it necessary to issue a direct appeal for calm to the general public in a
radio and television broadcast. 'Ulster stands at the crossroads',
he declared and continued:

Our conduct over the coming days and weeks will decide our

future ... These (issues) are far too serious to be determined behind closed doors or left to noisy minorities. The time has come for the people as a whole to speak in a clear voice ... Unionism armed with justice will be a stronger cause than Unionism armed merely with strength ... What kind of Ulster do you want? A happy and respected province in good standing with the rest of the United Kingdom? Or a place torn apart by riots and demonstrations and regarded by the rest of Britain as a political outcast?[6]

The Quarterly Meeting of the Carrickfergus Circuit of the MCI took place that evening. Rather fearfully, since this was my first such Circuit meeting and I had no idea how members might respond, I proposed that a telegram be sent to the Prime Minister expressing confidence in his leadership and support for his policies. A lively discussion followed, and rather to my surprise the proposal was approved unanimously. In the days following there was a vast outpouring of public support for the Prime Minister's speech from over 150,000 people through letters, telephone calls, telegrams and petitions. The day after O'Neill's broadcast a telegram was sent on behalf of the ICC Executive in the names of its officers, Dr Eric Gallagher, Principal James Haire, John Radcliffe and myself. It read, 'Pledging wholehearted support for call to prayer and aims outlined in broadcast.'

January to December 1969

Any hope of a lasting improvement in the atmosphere soon evaporated. On 1 January 1969, against the advice of NICRA, about forty members of the People's Democracy – a left-wing student group set up the previous October – began a four day march from Belfast to Derry. They were harried by loyalists at points along the road. By 4 January 1969 the number of marchers had risen to several hundred, accompanied by eighty policemen. At Burntollet Bridge near Derry, the marchers were viciously attacked by about two hundred loyalists including part-time off-duty policemen. Stones, sticks, iron bars and bottles were used in the attack, and thirteen marchers had to receive hospital treatment. Further serious disturbances followed after the marchers entered the city, with the police forcing their way into the staunchly republican Bogside area. It has been suggested

that the failure of the UUP government to handle this march better was arguably one of the gravest mistakes of the Troubles.
The episode further deepened hostility among Catholics towards the state, and created increased sympathy in favour of
human rights. At the same time questions remained about the
motivation, integrity and judgement of marchers. Fear deepened
within the majority.

A further meeting was convened on 8 January to prepare for
the proposed consultation between RC leaders, the leaders of
ICC member churches and representatives from the Council, to
which Archbishop James McCann (the Primate of the C of I), Dr
John Withers (the Moderator of the General Assembly) and
Gerald Myles (the Methodist President) were specially invited.
The meeting took three important initiatives. First, a confidential approach was made to Cardinal Conway of the RCC which
proved productive in both the short and long term, with the setting up of an unpublicised *ad hoc* Catholic/Protestant Committee which met first in April 1969, and an ICC/RCC Joint
Group launched two years later. These will be discussed in the
next chapter. Second, a statement was released to the press, with
sixteen signatories including the church leaders as named plus
Albert McElroy (the Non-Subscribing Presbyterian Moderator),
Joseph Cooper (of the Moravian Church), Lt Col George Snell (of
the Salvation Army), Norah Douglas (of the Religious Society of
Friends), and nine others including the officers of the Council.
This statement expressed 'profound disquiet and disapproval'
over the violence at Burntollet Bridge and within Derry, and
condemned 'unreservedly' the actions of those who claimed to
be motivated on behalf of their faith. 'Activity of this kind', the
statement ran, 'is in flagrant contradiction to the ... principles of
true Protestantism ... and is completely contrary to the mind
and will of our Lord Jesus Christ.' Third, a letter in the name of
the sixteen signatories was sent in confidence to Terence O'Neill
with a copy of the press release. The letter declared that the signatories unanimously favoured the appointing of a judicial inquiry, and requested the Prime Minister to bring their initiative
to the attention of the Cabinet. Suggestions as to the range an
inquiry should take were set out in detail:

We particularly request that ... an enquiry (sic) should address itself to the following points: (a) the composition and aims of the Civil Rights Movement, (b) the composition and aims of the Ulster Constitution Defence Committee, the Loyal Citizens of Ulster and other similar organisations, (c) the events in Londonderry leading up to and on October 5th, 1968, in Armagh ... on November 30th, 1968, and again in Londonderry ... on January 4th, 1969, (d) Government decisions connected with these events, and (e) instructions given to and actions taken by the police connected therewith.[7]

The Prime Minister later acknowledged that this approach had strengthened his hand in persuading reluctant members of the Cabinet of the need to set up the Cameron Commission.

O'Neill's position continued to be difficult. On 23 January Brian Faulkner, the Deputy Prime Minister who was opposed to an inquiry, resigned from the government. Days later another two senior UUP resignations took place, and 'the juggernaut of dissidence accelerated'. At the end of the month twelve Unionist backbenchers issued a demand for the removal of O'Neill in the interests of party unity. Ken (later Sir Kenneth) Bloomfield – O'Neill's trusted 'word-spinner and ideas' person – had this kind of sequence of events in mind when he admitted that 'the cabinet was not a collection of convinced reformers'. A regular pattern could be discerned within Unionism, with external demands for reform eventually leading to belated compromises which were no longer acceptable to anyone. 'In a rising market', Bloomfield commented, 'Unionism constantly tried, unsuccessfully, to buy reform at last year's prices.'[8]

Members of the Belfast Council of Churches revealed awareness of this trend when on 30 January they expressed concern that the government appeared to be adopting a 'go-slow' policy on reforms. The CCB therefore decided to send another statement to the press, forwarding it on this occasion to the television channels, the Secretary of the Cabinet and the Prime Minister (with a covering letter in the latter case). This statement spoke of the CCB's concern for the entire community and of its welcome for three developments, the appointment of a Commission of Inquiry into 'the root causes' of unrest, the establishing of a Commission to administer Derry, and planned changes in connection with local government and housing. The CCB was sure that the implementation of these policies would help to lessen bitterness and unrest, and would encourage trust and goodwill within Northern Ireland and Britain. It would, however, view 'with alarm' any tendency not to pursue these aims. The Prime Minister replied saying he was 'deeply touched' by this support.

Against this background, my wife Margaret and I took a personal and unpublicised initiative on 1 February. Becoming aware that Captain Austin Ardill – then a Methodist and our local member of parliament – was involved with others in attempts to remove the Prime Minister, we wrote privately to him and sent a copy of the letter to the Prime Minister. Since becoming Secretary of the ICC I had made it a point of keeping Captain Ardill informed of ICC and other Council of Churches' statements on Northern Ireland affairs, sending copies of statements when available and speaking directly to him as opportunity arose. On this occasion I enclosed the CCB's statement of 30 January and met him within days. In appealing to him to reconsider his position, we commented in the letter that it seemed that those who were seeking to undermine the position of the Prime Minister were doing so not, as they claimed, to protect Unionist party unity – in any case there were more important matters than UUP unity – but to oppose essential reforms and to further their own political agendas. More than thirty years later I learnt that just before our contact with Captain Ardill, Dr Gallagher had been 'got at' on 26 January 1969 by 'a well known' but unnamed 'Methodist business man' who claimed to be close to Stormont politicians of Cabinet rank opposed to O'Neill. This person made Gallagher aware that Ardill was feeling 'let down' by the MCI.[9]

In the event, O'Neill dissolved parliament on 3 February and called an election on 24 February. This became known as the 'crossroads election' in which many moulds were broken, with pro- and anti-reform Unionist candidates standing alongside Protestant Unionists, Nationalists and others. New names appeared as candidates including Ian Paisley who unsuccessfully challenged O'Neill, and John Hume who as an independent defeated Eddie McAteer, the Nationalist leader. Captain Ardill lost out to Anne Dickson (a strong supporter of the Prime Minister who in 1976 became the first woman leader of a N. I. political party). O'Neill emerged as the over-all winner, but he had not been able to isolate his critics as he had hoped. With Unionist opposition and protests continuing, he resigned as Prime Minister on 28 April 1969. James Chichester-Clark succeeded O'Neill on 1 May, and announced that he would continue O'Neill's reforming policies. Not surprisingly, however, many Catholics were unconvinced by talk of change by Unionists. Even when the rhetoric altered, they questioned whether life could ever be different under UUP rule.

Coincidentally the spring meeting of the ICC also took place on 1 May 1969, and the Council used the opportunity to urge the new Prime Minister to implement reforms. It encouraged him and his colleagues in government to deal with all basic causes of unrest which properly fell within their sphere of responsiblity, and to 'promote that justice for all sections of the community on which the achievement of peace depends.' Recognising that some causes of unrest lay outside the government's sphere of influence, the Council renewed earlier calls on churches and others to consider how 'as a matter of great urgency' they could contribute to the creation of 'social reconciliation'. It asked its own Executive Committee to initiate a study of the role the churches could and should play in Ireland. Dr Gallagher pointed out that biblical Protestantism and political Protestantism were not the same, and indeed that there was 'no necessary connection between the two'. Whereas political Protestantism had to do with exercising power, biblical Protestantism involved 'a way of life, a way of obedience, a way of love'. Indeed biblical Protestantism, he argued, could well demand that we 'call in question the aims and methods of a Protestant ascendancy' and that risks be taken for community peace and reconciliation.[10]

A month earlier, in a church service on national radio at Greenisland on Palm Sunday, I commented from a Christian point of view on events within the Province:

> We've had opposition politicians (in Northern Ireland) behaving in a scarcely responsible manner ... and hard-line (Unionist) politicians who are so impressed by the traditional strength of the ruling party as to be contemptuous of the rights of opposition parties and politicians ... Worst of all, we've had the growth of narrowly-based sectarian groups,

> masquerading as religious movements, whose supporters in-
> timidate opponents, apparently intent on nothing more than
> safe-guarding and advancing sectional interests.[11]

Jesus, I suggested, exercised his authority in quite different ways. Compulsion and coercion found no place in his armoury, and he made his appeal only through persuasion and love. Claims by evangelicals and others on behalf of Christ – that he brings peace and reconciliation – would ring true only if there was clear evidence in people's lives that Christ transforms attitudes and relationships.

Few bodies, the churches included, could escape blame for their share in the Troubles. The April 1969 issue of *Theology*, a monthly review published in London by the Society for Promoting Christian Knowledge (SPCK), carried a ten page article by R. P. McDermott entitled 'Church and State in Northern Ireland'. After serving for twelve years in parochial ministry in Ireland, the author had taken a position in Durham university as a lecturer in theology. The article was sharply critical of the record of the member churches of the ICC in response to the developing crisis in Northern Ireland. Prompted by positive reports in the national press in Britain in December 1968, in which Bishop Sansbury (the General Secretary of the BCC) and the BCC Executive Committee had warmly commended statements and initiatives by the ICC and its member churches, McDermott argued that the ICC's record did not merit praise. He was particularly critical of what he regarded as the shallowness of the social and theological analysis of the crisis by the Irish churches, and condemned them for their slowness in responding to issues such as injustice, sectarianism and church links with the Orange Order. Some felt that McDermott's points would have carried more weight if he had not left Ireland many years before. Dr Gallagher, Principal Haire and I replied on behalf of the ICC on 15 April in a way that respected the sensitivities and confidences involved in the ICC's political and other contacts (including those with the Cardinal). Welcoming McDermott's article as 'useful, significant and stimulating', we drew attention to matters which could be mentioned and about which McDermott would not have known, including the call to the N. I. Prime Minister to appoint a commission to inquire into root causes of the crisis.[12] The Council's printed report for 1968-9 acknowledged that the ICC and its member churches could not 'be exonerated from blame for the tragic situation that (had) developed', admitting that 'for far too long manifest grievances have been ignored, and sincerely held fears remained unexamined.' The report went on to point out that the Council had become increasingly concerned to speak and act constructively.

On 13 and 14 May, Alan Booth, the London-based Secretary of the Churches' Commission on International Affairs, and a minister of the MCI who had been Dr Gallagher's contemporary at Trinity College, Dublin, and at Edgehill College, paid a fact finding visit to Northern Ireland. He met politicians, church leaders and the officers of the ICC. The following year Booth was appointed Director of Christian Aid.

The Troubles worsened rapidly through the summer 1969, with serious riots following the Orange parades in July. On 12 August the traditional Apprentice Boys' parade round Derry's walls was accompanied by further rioting which escalated into 'the battle of the Bogside', with about a thousand police entering the Nationalist area with armoured vehicles and water cannon closely followed by Protestant mobs smashing windows. Inevitably the effect on community relations was highly damaging, creating, in the words of a local priest, 'a community in revolt', with any hope of restoring moderation or calm destroyed. On 13 August Jack Lynch – Ireland's Taoiseach (Prime Minister) – declared on television that since the Stormont government had lost control, the Irish government could 'no longer stand by and see innocent people injured and perhaps worse'. Irish army field hospitals would be set up near the border to treat victims, he announced. The N. I. government, long used to financial dependence on the Westminster government, now had to face the unpalatable truth that by itself it could not guarantee its citizens law and order. Its urgent request to London for help was accepted and British troops were sent in on 14 August. The political balance between Northern Ireland and London was fundamentally altered by this development, given that London would not accept Stormont control of the army, though this was not widely understood at the time.

At first the army was welcomed by Nationalists, who feared

the police more than the army. This reaction was not to last, however. Nationalists were alarmed and angry that the IRA had been weak and was unable to defend them. With trust eroding and bitter sectarian clashes breaking out across the Province, 'no-go' areas were declared in working-class districts. Hundreds of houses were burned, leaving thousands of people, mainly Catholics, homeless. The Prime Minister convened a series of thirteen peace conferences between 18 August and September, involving a wide variety of bodies including churches, trade unions, universities, Belfast Corporation, the Londonderry Development Commission, the N. I. Chamber of Commerce and Industry and others. The conferences were more than a cosmetic or PR exercise, with discussions focused on issues such as medical and other services in refugee centres, emergency financial provision, protection against intimidation and emergency housing.[13]

On 21 August Dr Jack Sayers, a committed Methodist and the respected and liberalising editor of the Province's largest-selling newspaper, the *Belfast Telegraph*, was so deeply shocked that he wrote to a friend to say he felt 'crushed by the human tragedy of it all'. Unionism, it seemed to him, had been indicted by events and might not recover. He for one sensed the ominous political significance of what was unfolding, and in describing developments resorted in a radio broadcast on 20 August to the use of the word 'blitz' with its associations with the second world war:

It wasn't exactly a revolution, although to the world it must have looked very like one. But it *was* the most shattering week, and the most earth-shaking politically, that Northern Ireland has known in all the fifty years of its stormy history … Eight people killed and millions of pounds' worth of property destroyed by fires that brought back awful memories of the blitz. We were a province in utter turmoil, gripped by communal fears and on the very brink of civil war that might have involved the Irish Republic too … Will it all work out? Is this the end of the great Civil Rights agitation that began last October? Can there really be peace and common purpose between Protestants and Catholics, Unionists and Nationalists? Is this the best way to hasten the political education so much neglected in the past? We can only hope it will, and that first of all Ulster ceases to be an armed camp ruled by fright ...[14]

Sayers did not live long enough to receive answers to his questions. Days later he died following a massive heart attack.

How did the churches respond to the deepening crisis? There was at the time 'a significant leadership vacuum'[15] within the C of I, with the resignation of Archbishop McCann and the imminent retirement of other senior Northern bishops. Before settling into life in Armagh, the newly appointed Archbishop of Armagh and Anglican Primate, Dr George Simms, wisely spent days walking the riot-torn streets of Belfast in the company of Canon Elliott, to observe the horror of the situation for himself. Church halls were opened to receive the homeless. Hasty attempts were made to provide counselling and practical support for frightened and homeless people. Local clergy met with police and community leaders, seeking to keep community factions apart and to prevent the situation from becoming worse. The leaders of the C of I, MCI, PCI and RCC (in time, as they met more frequently, they would simply become known as 'the four church leaders') appeared together on television for the first time on 1 September 1969, jointly expressing the hope that people would remain calm for a period of six weeks to allow promised reforms to be introduced.

An emergency meeting of the ICC Executive Committee took place on 18 August. Sympathy was expressed to all who had suffered in the disturbances, those who had lost homes or employment and particularly those whose loved ones had been killed or incurred injuries. Messages of concern and support poured in from the world church. One was received from the Central Committee of the WCC, meeting in Canterbury. It conveyed the assurance that the wider Christian family shared Ireland's pain and identified with the struggle 'for right and reconciliation'. The ICC Executive urged churches and the wider community to assist all victims of violence. It was encouraged by instances in which cross-community friendship and co-operation held fast, and commended church people and others who worked to create and maintain peace wherever possible. The Executive also welcomed the N. I. Prime Minister's announcement that peace conferences were to be called, and re-affirmed its own conviction that there could only be peace with justice for all.

The response in Downpatrick to an influx of refugees from Belfast, mainly Catholics, set an example for others to follow. Organised on an ecumenical basis, there was a reception centre for incoming refugees in the C of I parish hall, with dispersal centres in the Presbyterian hall and the Catholic scout hall. Food was provided by volunteers from a kitchen where school meals were normally prepared. A notice was read in local churches, requesting people with spare accommodation to make it available. The response was genuinely on a cross-community basis, and exceeded requirements.

Contacts took place with the British Council of Churches through its General Secretary, Bishop Kenneth Sansbury. Dr Gallagher took part in a meeting of the BCC Executive Committee in September, and addressed the BCC's full meeting in October in a debate on Northern Ireland. 'The battle for the mind and soul of Ulster is on', he warned, adding that 'it may be won or lost this winter.' A resolution was passed expressing appreciation of the positive lead given by the ICC and the BCC member churches in Ireland. It drew attention to reforms already promised by the UK and Northern Ireland governments, emphasised the importance of early implementation, and called for whatever further action was needed 'to create social and economic justice and permanent reconciliation among all' in Northern Ireland.

But who spoke for Protestantism in those dark days of fear, confrontation and deepening division? At an ICC Executive Committee in Dundalk on 17 October, reference was made to Ian Paisley's frequently repeated claim to speak on behalf of Protestants, as for example in a call for a mass lobby of protest at Stormont. The leaders of the three main Protestant churches issued a statement in which they asked people to remain at their places of work and not to give in to intimidation. The statement received support from the Trade Union movement. However, Paisley's 'incendiary rhetoric',[16] expressed in language calculated to appeal to frightened people concerned for their future and resistant to change, was the voice that demanded attention. Quieter, wiser words were spoken on behalf of the churches and in the interests of the entire community and its future, but they made less impact than they ought. For example, at the half-yearly meeting of the ICC in Belfast on 6 November, Dr Gallagher – about to step down as chairman – addressed the Council:

> The last six months have been easily the most momentous and dramatic in the history of Northern Ireland. The foundations of our Provincial and community life have been rocked and at times the structure of our society seemed in danger of collapse ... As a Council we welcome the declared intention of the government to press on with reforms ... I only wish that I could see more evidence of convinced and enthusiastic support coming from the government's backbenches ...By an act of courage and magnanimity the Protestant people of Ulster can do more for the good name and survival of Protestantism than all the built-in safeguards of a political ascendancy can provide. By an act of statesmanship and equal magnanimity the Catholic minority can find itself playing a full and satisfying part in all that makes our common life possible. Each must face the fears and grievances of the other. Is each or either side big enough for the challenge?[17]

A resolution similar to that agreed by the BCC the previous month, was passed with two additional clauses. The appointment of the first Minister of Community Relations – Dr Robert Simpson – was welcomed and the churches were urged to co-operate with his department. Second, a welcome was given to the news that leading representatives of some of the ICC member churches, together with Cardinal Conway, had been invited by the new Minister to discuss and report on 'religious misunderstanding and fears which cause concern, suspicion and division' in Northern Ireland.

January to December 1970

A new IRA, known as the 'Provisionals' in contrast to the 'Officials', was born in December 1969. A split along the same lines took place in the political wing, Sinn Féin, in January 1970. The Provisionals sought to provide vulnerable Catholic communities with protection against sectarian attacks, drew attention to what they saw as the fundamentally unfair and undemocratic nature of Northen Irish society, presented partition as maintaining an illegitimate state in the North and denying the right of national self-determination within Ireland as a whole, and portrayed the North as irreformable and therefore in need of force to achieve republican goals. An outline of Provisional IRA politics includes these points:

> Defence, defiance, retaliation and anti-imperialism were interwoven in their thinking; force would work, they believed, where conventional politics simply would not, and violent revolution was preferred to an impossible, peaceful reformism; contemporary conditions validated a lengthy republican tradition and orthodoxy; (and) Catholicism as well as socialism informed the organisation's thinking and identity ...[18]

Such principles and strategy involved the Provisionals in inevitable conflict with political opponents and with all who were willing to operate within the existing constitutional frameworks in Northern Ireland, Britain and the Republic of Ireland.

The rapid growth of the more militant Provisional IRA inevitably led to greatly increased levels of republican violence within the North and had a seriously unsettling effect throughout Ireland. Two senior cabinet ministers in the Republic, Charles Haughey and Neil Blaney, were dismissed by the Taoiseach, Jack Lynch, on 6 May and later arrested. They appeared in court on 28 May, charged in connection with the illegal importing of arms into the North. Rumours ran rife, for example of a threat to the Taoiseach's position, intervention in the North by the Republic and arms support for the Provisionals. Both former ministers were eventually cleared in the courts, Blaney in July and Haughey in October. Aspects of the crisis remain a mystery. 'There is now no doubt', concludes a recent study, 'that some money did go from the Dublin government to the proto-Provisionals' who by this time were committed to armed conflict with Britain.[19] Lynch survived the storm and his party, Fianna Fáil, entered a phase in which it re-thought its position on the nature of republicanism and the appropriateness of violence as a way of promoting its goals.

The Conservatives, led by Edward Heath, came to power in the general election of 18 June, with Ian Paisley elected as MP for North Antrim. On 27 June serious rioting took place in north and east Belfast, with five Protestants and one Catholic shot dead. The following day five hundred Catholic workers were expelled by Protestants from the shipyard in East Belfast. On 1 July Reginald Maudling visited Northern Ireland for the first time as Home Secretary, and was heard to remark on his return flight to London, 'What a bloody awful country!' To facilitate a search for weapons in the Catholic Lower Falls area of Belfast, a curfew lasting thirty-four hours was imposed on 3 July, with a break for a few hours to allow for shopping and other necessary movement. Considerable damage was caused to hundreds of homes, and three men were shot dead by the army while a fourth was crushed by an army vehicle. None of the four had been IRA activists. The curfew marked a serious worsening in relations between the Catholic working class and the army. Sectarian violence also continued, forcing many people from their homes including Protestants from the mixed but mainly Catholic New Barnsley estate. In these circumstances a family of four from New Barnsley shared our home in Greenisland for some days. Before long there was talk of the largest displacement of civilian population in Europe since the second world war, through the forced removal of families (mainly Catholics) in the Belfast area.

I wrote to the Primate, the Moderator and the President on 9 April 1970, following a meeting of the ICC Executive Committee in Dundalk, requesting them 'to seek a joint, personal and unpublicised meeting' with the leaders of the Orange Order, to discuss the worsening situation in the community and preparations for the twelfth of July parades. If there was any prospect of the parades being cancelled or curtailed, to avoid further community unrest, early action would be necessary so that the organisers could avoid incurring heavy financial losses. If a successful meeting took place, my letter continued, perhaps the church leaders could consider contacting the Cardinal to see if he would discuss Nationalist marches with the leaders of the Ancient Order of Hibernians.[20] The Executive used this indirect approach, recognising that even a low key and unpublicised initiative by the ICC might be misunderstood because of the suspicion in which the ecumenical movement was held.

Archbishop Simms and Jack Weir (the Clerk or General

Secretary of the PCI, who was to receive an honorary doctorate in 1972) reported on this initiative at the May meeting of the Executive. The three church leaders, with Weir, had met six representatives of the Orange Order, one from each of the counties in Northern Ireland. The Orangemen had expressed hurt at what they described as sustained criticism of the Order by the churches, claiming that they believed the Order exercised a steadying influence in the country. It was felt that the churches and others had not shown sufficient understanding of people's frustrations and problems through times of change. For example, in the Shankill Road area of Belfast there was much evidence of urban decay and deterioration and little sign of planning or improvements, which inevitably led to frustration and anger. The church leaders had promised to speak to the Minister of Development about this, and were able to report to the Executive that this contact had already been made. Regarding the 1970 parades, the Orange leaders felt that these ought to be allowed to proceed since arrangements were already in place. If they did not go ahead they might be replaced by unofficial demonstrations which could be more difficult to steward. Everything possible would be done to prevent trouble, the Orange leaders had assured them.

In the discussion which followed it was clear that members of the Executive were divided as to whether contacts with the Loyal Orders should continue. Some felt that they might lead to useful dialogue in which, for example, Orange misperceptions and fears about the ecumenical movement could be addressed. Others, however, expressed misgivings, suspecting that the talks might be misrepresented, achieve little and damage the Council. At the June meeting of the Executive it was agreed to take no further action on this front though it was recognised that individuals might keep lines of communication open.

On 29 May the Macrory Report on the reform of local government was completed. It abolished an old system of local government based on the six counties, and replaced it with twenty-six district councils. Area boards were set up to administer health, education and library sevices. The Unionist government accepted the recommendations in December. The intention behind the changes was that the N. I. parliament would run these newly centralised services, but with the introduction of direct rule in 1972 the control of services, including the power to nominate members to the boards, passed to the Secretary of State and his ministers. This greatly reduced the powers of new district councils, restricting their influence to what was disparagingly described as 'bins, bogs and burials', and left locally elected representatives with a frustrating sense of powerlessness.

'Your God or your gun', was the challenge presented in a sermon in the Grosvenor Hall by Dr Gallagher on Sunday 12 July. He spoke of reforms without reformation, a peace line which was really a battle line, a bitter Ulster instead of a better one, a Northern Ireland which young people wanted to leave rather than one in which they wanted to live, and the most religious country in the world now become infamous because of the blasphemy of its violence. His appeal to politicians was stark. 'Are you for God and your fellow men, or do you want the gun and the end of all hope?'[21] On 23 July the Stormont government banned processions until January 1971, in a bid to reduce tension.

A Ministry of Community Relations had been created in 1969, on the initiative of James Callaghan then Home Secretary. This followed a commitment in a joint communique by the British and N. I. governments to designate a Minister with responsibility in the area of community relations in Northern Ireland. Dr Robert Simpson, a Unionist MP, was the first person appointed. Nine groups, mainly church-related, met at Stormont on 28 July 1970 with Dr Simpson and members of staff from his department. These were the Irish Association; the Fellowship of Prayer (represented by the Redemptorist priest, Alec Reid, later a key figure in the process leading to the Good Friday Agreement in 1998); the Fellowship of Reconciliation (represented by Denis Barritt of the Religious Society of Friends); the Peace Committees (represented by David Bleakley, G. B. Newe and Dr Gallagher); PACE (Protestant and Catholic Encounter); Platform (represented by Desmond Wilson, a Catholic priest); the Religious Society of Friends; the Voluntary Service Bureau; and the ICC (represented by myself).

Each group indicated its main areas of interest and activity. Points to emerge in the discussions included funding, leader-

ship training, perspectives and attitudes, the media and communication, 'grass roots' community work, responses to conflict sit-
uations in other countries, and the need to share ideas and to
make programmes and plans more widely known across the
community. I drew attention to increasing co-operation between
the ICC and the RCC. The Minister emphasised the need for
'law and order' to be restored, so that long-term resolutions to
social and community problems could be found. A feasibility
study would be carried out on areas of concern relevant to the
activity of the groups, with a field worker appointed by the
Community Relations Commission. Lack of private funding
would not be allowed to prevent essential programmes proceeding, assured the Minister. It was agreed that there was value
in the various organisations and the Ministry of Community
Relations keeping in touch.

The Community Relations Commission had also been appointed in 1969, with Maurice Hayes, a Roman Catholic, as its
first chairman. Like the Ministry, this too came about as a result
of Westminster pressure on the N. I. government. Not having
given a thought to community relations for the previous fifty
years, as Hayes put it, the Unionists now found themselves with
a Minister, a Ministry and a Commission. Stormont, he claimed,
was not at all sure what to do with them, or what their respec-
tive roles and relationships were to be.[22] Ministers tended to operate in their own way, each bringing his own gifts, interests and
experience to the job. The Commission, for its part, assembled a
team of professional field workers – people of varied backgrounds, disciplines and political outlooks – committed to
working together in developing local community leadership in
areas such as non-violent ways of resolving conflict.

Bishop Sansbury of the BCC sought to keep in close contact
with the developing political and community situation in
Northern Ireland. From the latter part of 1969 he had an
Advisory Group with which to consult for this purpose. Its ini-
tial members were Arthur Macarthur, the Chairman of the
BCC's Administrative Committee; Hugh Wilcox, the Secretary
of the Joint International Department of the BCC and the
Conference of British Missionary Societies; and John Hough, the
Secretary of the BCC's Social Responsibility Department. This

group visited Northern Ireland in the autumn 1970, meeting church leaders, politicians, trade unionists, army and police staff, and community leaders 'on the ground'. In time the advisory group was strengthened, with the addition of others including David Bleakley (a former NILP MP at Stormont) and Sean Nolan (Deputy Principal of St Joseph's College of Education, Belfast).

Sansbury occasionally received expressions of concern from local Councils of Churches and others in Britain about the worsening situation in Ireland. These were well-intentioned but not necessarily well-informed. One, in October 1970, urged the BCC 'to take action to bring back peace into Northern Ireland'. In this case the gathering crisis was viewed in simplistic terms. 'The disorders ... are mainly due to hostility between two portions of the Christian Churches', the resolution ran. Its suggested way forward was 'to call for the mounting of a massive Crusade to (bring) the contestants back to their fundamental loyalty to Jesus Christ and to love for their neighbours'. The reference to a crusade, though presumably not intended in an historical sense, was particularly insensitive. In his reply Bishop Sansbury referred to the role of his Advisory Group, and indicated that there was a problem with rioters who were 'tribally' Protestant or Catholic, but who really had 'no religious allegiance at all' (much like skinheads in Britain, he suggested). 'Only violence' was considered 'telegenic', the bishop wrote in reply, adding that initiatives were being taken by churches and others in Ireland in attempts to promote justice, reconciliation and peace.[23]

Earlier, in the summer 1970, the ICC received a letter from M. A. Z. Rolston, General Secretary of the National Christian Council of India, which suggested that the conflict in Ireland was perceived in other parts of the world as an obstacle to Christian witness. Wide publicity was given to the letter in both the church and secular press:

> We do not need to remind you that events in your country have major repercussions in India and the rest of the world ... (These events) inevitably affect the witness that we as Indian Christians are endeavouring to make among our fellow-citizens of other faiths, and we feel bound to point out that a prolonging of the conflict will gravely damage the

cause of Christ's kingdom throughout the world and not least in those countries where the Gospel of the redeeming grace and power of Christ is being proclaimed in a non-Christian environment ... We implore you to make every effort towards reconciliation ... Please pray for us. God grant that you and we may be made 'instruments of His peace' in the midst of a turbulent world.[24]

A useful correspondence followed between Mr Rolston and myself. Principal Haire and the Archbishop of Dublin, Alan Buchanan, were able to speak directly to Indian and other national church leaders when they attended the inauguration of the Church of North India in November 1970.

January to December 1971

In January 1971 the split between the Official and Provisional IRA spilled on to the streets, with the Provisionals gaining control in most parts of nationalist Belfast. Under the Police Act of March 1970, the N. I. government had accepted and acted upon the principle of 'a civilianised and unarmed police force'. Two unarmed policemen were killed by the IRA on 26 February in Belfast, effectively ending any hope that 'the RUC could operate as an unarmed "English Bobby" style police force', in the view of Brian Faulkner.[25] The first policeman to be killed in the Troubles had, however, been shot in October 1969 by the UVF, an illegal Protestant paramilitary force. On 28 February 1971 members of the RUC were issued with flak jackets and bullet proof vests. Days later the police in some areas were reissued with guns, partly for self protection. On 9 March three off-duty soldiers including two brothers, aged 17 and 18, were killed near Belfast. The N. I. Prime Minister, Chichester-Clark, resigned on 20 March in protest at what he regarded as an inadequate security response by the British government to the deteriorating situation. Brian Faulkner succeeded as Prime Minister. David Bleakley, a former NILP MP at Stormont, became Minister of Community Relations on 16 March. Not then an MP, he was only entitled under the Government of Ireland Act to serve for a maximum of six months.

On 1 April Dr Gallagher was featured prominently in the pages of the London-based weekly, the *Methodist Recorder*. The headlines drew attention to the deteriorating situation in Northern Ireland, 'Mad March Days in Ulster', 'IRA policy' and 'Strangle hold'. There was still some hope, according to Gallagher, just 'a very few rays of light', but time was fast running out. It was around this time that he began to focus on 'Ten Commandments for Peacemakers'. Not set in stone or polished, they were an attempt in a time of crisis to be personal, direct and practical, and are given, as Gallagher would have done, in an informal rather than a literary form. First, root out hatred and bitterness wherever you find them. Second, talk up anything good and hopeful. There are too many prophets of gloom. Third, don't believe or spread every rumour. Fourth, support people who work for peace based on justice. Fifth, keep your children off the streets when there's trouble. Sixth, plan and work to make your neighbourhood cleaner and brighter. Seventh, ask yourself why 'the other side' says what it does say. Eighth, don't repeat gossip. Ninth, invite 'the other side' to your home to find out what makes it 'tick'. Ten, make your slogan 'the best for the whole community, not just what's best for me.'[26]

In May 1969 the ICC had welcomed the publication of a report by the (British) Evangelical Alliance's Commission on Evangelism (EA), entitled *On the Other Side*, and commended it for study. Mission, the EA report had claimed, is 'the total activity of God in reconciling individuals to himself and in transforming society.' What might this mean for churches in Ireland immersed in the Troubles? The ICC Executive set up a working party to consider the relevance of the material for Ireland under the chairmanship of Victor Lynas, who became Moderator of the Presbyterian Assembly in June 1972.

In its report 'Evangelism in Northern Ireland Today' presented to the ICC on 15 April 1971, the working party highlighted points relevant to the presentation of the gospel in a society in which 'sectarian bitterness' and a form of 'organised religion' wedded at times to the political *status quo*, were prominent elements:

> Disdain for restraint and contempt for authority are twin features of Ulster life which we must not dismiss lightly ... In some sense the social quagmire and political jungle of the Province are an indictment of the Church, which still retains

contact with a large segment of the populace. We have failed
to send out into every part of society men and women committed to Christian ideals, who are prepared to demonstrate
the relevance of the Gospel to the whole of life ... Over and
above the words we use, we must mediate to others the presence of the living Christ, so that there may be personal encounter, the rapport between man and God ... By offering
friendship, by winning confidence, by sharing interests, by
genuine caring, we must learn to speak the truth in love.[27]

On 13 June 1971 Orangemen defied a ban and marched through
a mainly Catholic village, Dungiven. This led to a clash with the
army and police, ending with the use of rubber bullets and CS
gas. Contact with the Orange Order was again raised at the ICC
Executive meeting on 23 June, when I introduced a letter from
Bishop Sansbury in which he reported British comments on the
Order. This sparked a lively debate in which widely differing
views were expressed. John Armstrong, the Bishop of Cashel,
spoke of English people 'dabbling' in something 'they knew
nothing about'. Carrie Barnett (later Carrie Barkley and a Vice-
President of the BCC), a Presbyterian educationist who worked
at Presbyterian headquarters, felt that perhaps representatives
from the Order should be invited to address the Council on the
Order's role in society. Dean Lillie spoke of 'a strong leaven of
sense' within the Order, with members of the clergy exercising a
moderating influence. Robert Nelson (a former President of the
MCI who had served for many years in Ceylon) questioned
why, if the latter claim was true, wiser statements on community
issues were not forthcoming from the Order.

On 22 June, the fiftieth anniversary of the Stormont parliament, Faulkner announced a plan to involve all parties in three
parliamentary committees to review policy and advise on legislation, two of the committees to be chaired by opposition MPs.
The SDLP gave an initial welcome, but the proposal was soon
overtaken by events on the streets. After the deaths of two men
in disputed circumstances in Derry, John Hume made an unsuccesful call for an impartial inquiry. The SDLP withdrew from
Stormont in protest on 16 July, and set up its own short-lived
'Assembly of the Northern Irish People'. Much more effective
from a Nationalist point of view was a long-running campaign

of civil disobedience, involving the non-payment of rents and rates and the withdrawal of Catholics from public office.

Against a background of continuing IRA violence and growing fears of a Protestant backlash, and despite nationalist warnings of outright opposition to internment without trial – though Faulkner claimed that 'secret representations from responsible members of the Catholic community prominent in politics' had urged him to 'lock up' those who were making life 'intolerable for ordinary Catholics'[28] – internment was introduced. In the first series of swoops in the night of 8 to 9 August, 342 men were arrested, all thought to be republicans associated mainly with the Official IRA. This latter point, that all the first internees were republican suspects, was not at first widely known. Many mistakes were made in implementing internment, and within two days 105 of those arrested were released. From the South, Jack Lynch commented that the introduction of internment was 'deplorable evidence of the political poverty of Ulster's policies'. Internment was seen by many in N. I. and Britain as 'a last throw of the dice', a frontal attack on the IRA and an attempt to ward off the threat of a violent backlash against republicanism from within the majority community. An N. I. official wrote that those involved in its introduction were well aware that the stakes were high, and that failure to reduce violence would inevitably result in fundamental changes.

In fact internment led to a huge escalation in violence throughout the Province. By 12 August twenty-two people had been killed, including a Catholic priest, Hugh Mullan, shot while administering the last rites in a riot situation in Belfast on 9 August. A second Catholic priest, Noel Fitzpatrick, was to die in similar circumstances a year later on 9 July. Up to 7,000 people were left homeless following the introduction of internment, the majority of them Catholics, some thousands fleeing to refugee camps in the Republic. Protestants were forced out of Belfast's Ardoyne district, women and children coming under machine-gun fire as they vacated their homes. About 200 houses were deliberately torched to prevent them being occupied by Catholics. In time it was widely acknowledged that internment had been 'poorly conceived, badly executed and markedly counter-productive'.[29] Major factors in its failure were the inaccuracy of police intelligence, the one-sidedness of its initial implementation against republicans, and the alleged treatment of internees. The Provisional IRA were the main beneficiaries, with levels of recruitment soaring. As unrest and violence increased, William Craig and Ian Paisley addressed a crowd of almost 20,000 people in Victoria Park, Belfast, on 6 September, demanding that a 'third force' be formed to defend Ulster. On 12 September Cardinal Conway and five Catholic bishops denounced the IRA and criticised internment. 'Who in their sane senses', the Cardinal asked, 'wants to bomb a million Protestants into a united Ireland?'[30]

What of the response to internment within the ICC and its member churches? A statement on internment was issued on the evening of Monday 9 August by the C of I Archbishop of Armagh, the Moderator of the PCI and the President of the MCI, following a hastily convened and extraordinary meeting of the unpublicised *ad hoc* Committee on Community Relations. The names of those holding these offices in the churches were not, however, always included in the media coverage of the statement, for reasons that will become plain.[31] The statement referred to the high level of violence and bloodshed within the community, for which there could be no justification from a Christian point of view; recognised that the government 'in its duty to all citizens (had) no option but to introduce strong measures which must be distasteful to many'; regretted 'the necessity for the introduction of internment'; noted the provision of an appeals' process 'designed to safeguard the rights of law abiding citizens'; called for restraint in holding legitimate peaceful demonstrations in the present dangerous circumstances, in the interests of 'the true well being of the whole community'; welcomed 'the acceptance of the government's decision' banning marches by those planning 'the march proposed for Thursday next' (a reference to the Apprentice Boys' parade in Derry); and welcomed too 'the Prime Minister's urgent call to all the people in Northern Ireland to play their part' in working for the good of the country. 'Violence and fear are the enemy of us all', the statement continued, concluding with a call for 'persistent prayer by everybody'.[32]

In the Republic, both Catholics and Protestants were highly

critical of the statement, much of the criticism being directed against Archbishop Simms, the former Archbishop of Dublin. In the North also, many regretted the statement. Invited by the *Methodist Recorder* to comment on the situation in the community in the immediate aftermath of internment, Harold Sloan remarked that it was 'hell on earth'. The WCC responded quickly. The day after internment I received a telegram from Dr Carson Blake, the General Secretary of the WCC, informing me that he had contacted the leaders of the WCC member churches in Ireland, together with the Catholic Primate (the contact was 'indirect' in the latter case), to express concern at the deteriorating situation and to say that the WCC stood ready 'to facilitate any ecumenical and peace making effort' the church leaders considered 'constructive and possible'. Could I co-ordinate responses, he asked?

An emergency meeting of the ICC Executive Committee was convened on 13 August in Belfast, with several members unable to attend due to their absence on holiday. The poor attendance greatly limited what could be done, and in the circumstances most attention focused on the WCC initiative. Dr Jack Weir reported that the Executive of the Presbyterian Government Committee had considered the matter and had concluded that a WCC initiative would be counter-productive. The Moderator of the General Assembly had already replied to Dr Blake and had referred to the embarrassment caused by the widespread publicity given to the WCC telegram before its receipt by WCC member churches. Weir also emphasised the difference between responses by WCC member churches and the ICC. Did he mean that a response from the Council would carry less weight, or that it would be taken less seriously, or that it would be improper, or ... ? Archbishop Simms commented that a reply from the C of I would await consultation between him and the Secretary of the Church's Unity Committee. Dr Gallagher was unaware if the telegram had yet been received by the Methodist Church.

In discussion it emerged that the Presbyterians were considering a fact-finding visit by the WCC 'without publicity'.This was being explored directly with Dr Blake. Dr Gallagher said he had been approached by Catholics about 'possible WCC mediation' in Northern Ireland. His own view was that a mediator needed the confidence of both sides, and that the WCC was not in this position. He felt that a WCC delegation could be invited, but only with a carefully agreed and restricted agenda. The WCC and its member churches in Ireland could benefit from such an initiative, if properly prepared and presented. I introduced two related matters. First, a WCC study on violence and non-violence worldwide had been initiated, in connection with which a WCC staff member would be visiting Northern Ireland in September. Second, at a meeting in Geneva in July in which I had met members of the WCC's Development Commission, the question of possible help for rehabilitation projects in Ireland had been raised. Was there, I wondered, a case for five or six representatives from the Irish churches going to Geneva in this connection, to meet staff members from different WCC departments to take discussions forward? The Chairman, Principal James Haire, was soon to visit Geneva and was asked to bear these points in mind during his discussions.

Another ICC Executive meeting was held in Dublin on 10 September, when a proposal was made that the Committee should formally disassociate itself from the inter-church statement of 9 August.This proposal and the speech proposing it had been circulated to members prior to the meeting. It presented the Committee with a major dilemma. Could it distance itself from a statement associated with the three largest member churches of the Council? What might be the consequences of such a step? Since the proposer of the motion, Barry Deane – a prominent C of I layman from Bandon, county Cork – was unavoidably absent from the meeting due to fog, and the proposal failed to attract a seconder, it was decided not to 'put' the proposal formally to the meeting but to discuss it none the less.

Deane's written speech[33] pulled no punches, describing the churches' statement as 'at best a gross error of judgement and at worst a colossal blunder.' It could, he argued, be said to call into question the Council's 'political impartiality' in the vital area of its work for reconciliation, though he noted and welcomed the fact that the statement had not been signed on behalf of the Council. Deane sought to impugn the statement on four grounds. First, it appeared to align the churches with a particular political party in the North. Second, it seemed to place the

churches alongside 'the Establishment', of which law and order
– inevitably viewed in a divided society in terms of party politics
– were the hall-mark. The churches' concern, Deane insisted,
ought rather to be on behalf of justice and morality. Third, the
church leaders' statement failed to take account of the likely
repercussions of internment. In this connection Deane pointed
to increased violence involving a higher death rate and greater
destruction of property, allegations of brutality against internees, violations of human rights and dignity, and the withdrawal of Catholics in greater numbers from public office in the
North. Fourth, the statement did not take adequate account of
the fact that the churches covered two political jurisdictions in
Ireland. Internment had been widely rejected within the
Republic, which in turn put at risk the goodwill between
Protestants and Catholics on which the role and safety of the
Protestant minority in the South largely depended.

In discussion it emerged that the statement had not in fact
been drawn up by the church leaders themselves but by 'appointed and authorised substitutes' acting on their behalf in
their absence, in a hastily convened meeting of the *ad hoc*
Committee on Community Relations without Catholic involvement. John Radcliffe, representing the smaller ICC member
churches, had not attended either. Widely differing views were
expressed and questions asked in the discussion at the ICC
Executive. Had the church leaders – including the Cardinal –
and others been consulted before the statement was released?
Was there now a split between the Protestant churches and the
Roman Catholic Church on internment, and indeed between
Northern and Southern elements within ICC member churches?
Attention has already been drawn to the fact that Cardinal
Conway and five Catholic bishops publicly criticised internment
days after its introduction. 'Intelligence' within Protestant
church circles would surely have indicated that this was likely
to happen. Robert Nelson described the joint statement as weak
and misleading, giving the impression that the three main
Protestant churches supported internment. Dean Lillie felt that
the threat of a loyalist/ Protestant backlash to IRA violence
formed part of the background to the introduction of internment. It was no bluff, and since internment gave some protec-

tion against a backlash, its introduction should be welcomed on that account. I informed the meeting of the thinking of a member of the Executive unable to be present, that the *ad hoc* Committee should not function in the absence of its Catholic members.

Dr Gallagher, a member of both the Executive and the *ad hoc* Committee, had the unenviable task of responding to the many concerns and questions raised in this highly charged debate. He reminded members of the speed at which events had moved immediately before and after the introduction of internment. He spoke too of pressure from the Ministry of Community Relations, for public support to be expressed for the ban on all marches. This ban, he said, had been imposed as 'a kind of counter-weight to internment'. There had been real fears lest even more widepread violence would follow if the ban had been ignored. The Apprentice Boys' parade in Derry presented an early and dangerous test. Urgent but unsuccessful attempts had been made to share a draft statement with church leaders and with members of the *ad hoc* Committee, including Catholics, he reported. For example Patrick Walsh, a Catholic member, had been visiting his mother in Andersonstown where he had become 'a virtual prisoner' in that no-one had been able to move in or out of the area. Eventually the wording had been finalised in most difficult circumstances, evolving through four drafts against a background of gunfire and explosions from the nearby Lower Falls district. Gallagher argued that the statement did not welcome internment and that it committed neither the signatories' churches nor the ICC. No-one at the meeting on 9 August was happy that internment had been introduced, he insisted. Those responsible for the statement had been unaware that only republican suspects had been interned, believing that internment had been introduced 'right across the board'. Important details had only came to light after the event. Had they been known earlier, a better statement could have been issued.

Deane's proposal was not put to the meeting of the ICC Executive for the reasons given, and there the matter rested. Many questions remain, for which we are unlikely ever to find fully satisfying answers, given the passage of time and the fact that only the Catholic members of the *ad hoc* Committee survive. Patrick Walsh had been invited to the meeting of the *ad hoc*

Committee but was unable to attend, as already noted. He was however contacted by telephone during the day. Denis Faul was not invited. Gallagher in his private papers speaks of 'repeated' and 'unsuccesful' attempts to get in touch. No direct contact was made with Cardinal Conway in Armagh, though in his private papers Gallagher indicates that he believed Patrick Walsh had been able to outline the statement to him by telephone. It would however have been clear to the members of the *ad hoc* Committee that the Cardinal would not have agreed to become a signatory to a statement which appeared to accept the necessity for the introduction of internment. As already noted, the Cardinal, with the other Northern bishops, publicly criticised internment a few days later. Why, one wonders, produce a statement at all when clearly circumstances militated against getting it right? Bishop Walsh has spoken of the pressure put on those who attended the meeting, or who were contacted in connection with it, to reach agreement by 9.00 pm at the latest.[34] Why such haste apart from the obvious point of wanting to catch the late night news on radio and television? Some have speculated that perhaps the government had applied pressure of a kind and intensity greater than was necessary to obtain support for the ban on marches. If so, for what reason and on what grounds? Dr Gallagher, as so often, was a central figure on the day. He appears to have taken the lead in convening the meeting and assisting the drafting process, and he provided the meeting place, the Grosvenor Hall. A person of great strength, sound judgement and the utmost integrity, one cannot see him easily yielding, or asking others to yield, to improper pressures from whatever source. The speed of events was rapid, communication difficult, details surrounding the introduction of internment unclear, and the dangers real. In such critical and extreme circumstances, errors of judgment were almost certain to take place. Dr Gallagher later admitted that he did not think he 'ever was party to a statement that caused so much agonising or gave so much difficulty.'[35] With the benefit of hindsight and on reflection, he greatly regretted the inclusion of the phrase 'the necessity for the introduction of internment', which clouded the issue and implied support. His private papers speak of 'the bungling of the whole operation' of internment. In time loyalist suspects were interned, and in 1975 Protestants and Catholics belatedly united in opposing detention without trial.

At the Executive Committee on 13 August, it had been agreed to seek a meeting with the Taoiseach, Mr Jack Lynch, to discuss the implications of statements he had made following internment and other issues. The deputation was chosen from those attending the Executive that day – the Chairman, Principal James Haire; Dr Gallagher; Cecil Hyland; Brian McConnell; David Poole; and myself. In the event, two were not able to meet the Taoiseach, Dr Gallagher and Brian McConnell. This was the first in a series of meetings with politicians. Initally no publicity was given to the meetings outside ICC circles. Archbishop George Simms was included in the deputation on becoming ICC Vice-Chairman. Cecil Hyland had to withdraw in the course of the series of interviews. The meeting with the Taoiseach took place on August 20, and was followed by a letter to him from me on 28 August. Follow-up letters became a regular feature after meetings, providing an opportunity to reiterate important points and on occasions to take matters further in the light of developments. These letters became a useful record of the conversations.[36]

Topics discussed with the Taoiseach included concern at the withdrawal of opposition MPs from Stormont, together with the nationalist campaign of civil disobedience. In the view of the ICC deputation, these policies had a seriously destabilising effect and contributed to polarisation between northern Catholics and Protestants at a time when the N. I. government – despite right-wing opposition within its own ranks – had 'set its face in the direction of reform'. The right of Roman Catholics to play their part in many areas of life had never been so widely recognised, the deputation argued, admitting at the same time that reforms should have been introduced earlier and gone further, and that the momentum for change needed to be kept up. Failure to acknowledge progress and to encourage those responsible for introducing it, they emphasised, would greatly strengthen the hand of the opponents of reform – including Protestant extremists – who wanted to resist change and to put the clock back. There were still moderate Protestants, Unionists included, who would continue to strive to find 'effective instruments of co-operation with their fellow-citizens who are Roman Catholics', the deputation claimed. Those committed to reform were, however, increasingly coming under pressure. Isolated already from elements within their own community, there was now the danger of them becoming isolated from moderate Catholics. Could the Taoiseach find ways of encouraging Unionist moderates? The hope was expressed that he would re-examine his own support for withdrawal and civil disobedience, and that he would bring the concerns of the deputation to the attention of those who were promoting these policies.

Significantly, the deputation touched lightly on the possibility of Irish unity by consent at some point in the future. For this to happen, a different approach on the part of successive Taoiseachs would be necessary. They would have to make it clear that they were interested not solely, or even primarily, 'in the welfare and objectives of only a minority of citizens in the North'. A genuine concern for all would have to be displayed 'if re-unification by consent' was to happen.

The recognition of how difficult it was to gain a true picture of events in Northern Ireland – due to limited cross-community contact and biased coverage by the media – led the deputation to question how well informed the Taoiseach was. Was he in touch with moderate Protestant opinion as well as moderate Catholic opinion, with non-Unionist parties other than the SDLP and the Nationalist Party, and with trade-unionists and business people as well as politicians? The members of the delegation readily admitted that they and others in Northern Ireland regularly suffered from too little contact with people who differed from themselves. This meeting with the Taoiseach was seen as important alongside other contacts, given the arms crisis in the Republic the previous year. It recognised the Taoiseach's special role in helping Fianna Fáil towards a form of republicanism in which the national question was to be resolved only by political and peaceful means.

The deputation next met with the SDLP. Principal James Haire, Brian McConnell (a Presbyterian minister) and I met Gerry Fitt in a Dublin hospital in which he was a patient, on 16 September. A letter followed on 22 September. The ICC deputation was not the only people with whom Gerry (later Lord) Fitt held court from his hospital bed. Maurice Hayes has described a similar scene around the same time, involving Conor Cruise O'Brien, Garret FitzGerald, a person from the British embassy, Hayes himself and 'a constantly changing retinue of visitors'.[37] A follow-up letter summarised the main points touched on by the ICC group including, first, the rapid deterioration within the majority community:

> The IRA campaign of violence and propaganda, the inability of the Security Forces to restore peace and to secure witnesses against terrorist suspects, and the programme of civil disobedience and non-participation are all combining to persuade greatly increasing numbers of people among the majority (not just the right-wing) that they are in a state of physical siege and that the minority will be satisfied with nothing less than the destruction of Northern Ireland. However inaccurate a reading of the situation this may be, it is strongly believed.

The talk among many within the majority was therefore of people preparing 'to deal with the other side before they destroy us'. Second, in these circumstances it was vital, argued the deputation, that responsible politicians on all sides sit down and talk to one another. At the start talks could simply be about talks, but they should then proceed as quickly as possible to consider 'the details of a fair and just settlement' to enable 'all who are prepared to work within a reformed Northern Ireland framework' to do so. Third, if as Mr Fitt himself had suggested in their conversation, 'the border could be taken out of politics' for a limited period, this could help to ease the present critical situation. Would it be possible for him and the SDLP to indicate in some open way, and without compromising their long-term political objectives, their willingness 'to participate in a re-structured Northern Ireland'? If so, a halt might be called to 'the present alarming slide towards violence'.

A meeting took place with John Hume at a venue near Derry on 20 September. Dr Gallagher, David Poole of the Religious Society of Friends and I represented the deputation. A letter was sent on 22 September, to underline the main points and to comment further. First, the members of the deputation emphasised that they had gone to the meeting 'at the behest and with the knowledge of no outside person or group of persons'. They belonged to no particular political party nor did they represent one. They acted only at the request of the ICC Executive Committee and would report only to them, in confidence. Second, their only concern in making the present series of contacts was to see 'responsible politicians engage in constructive discussion and negotiation'. They did this in the urgent belief that the longer 'the present impasse' continued, the greater the danger of civil war. Third, the deputation emphasised 'the marked change' that it discerned within 'the majority of the majority', which had become convinced that the Catholic minority did not want Northern Ireland to work and was determined to destroy it. This was tragic, argued the deputation, given that Mr Hume and others within the SDLP took a much more realistic line and exerted a moderating influence. The fact that the SDLP had withdrawn from Stormont before, rather than after, the introduction of internment, did however strengthen a conviction within the majority that the Catholic minority wanted to undermine the Province. If the SDLP could make it clear that they were prepared to participate within a restructured Northern Ireland without compromising their long-term political ideals, it might still be possible 'to convince many of the majority' that this was their position. Fourth, Mr Hume's reference to 'the bluff of the right wing' as a strategy occasionally resorted to by Unionists in an attempt to block reforms, had been noted. The deputation, however, believed that things had progressed far beyond this point, and that the situation was now much more threatening. Fifth, there had been reference in their conversation to making a fresh start in Northern Ireland after a period of 'rule by commission'. It was their judgement that even if such a proposal had been acceptable in the past, it would not now work. It was, they said, likely to be resisted 'to the limit'. 'You know what that implies', they added.

A deputation of six members – Principal James Haire, Dr Gallagher, Cecil Hyland, Brian McConnell, David Poole and I – met Brian Faulkner, the Prime Minister of Northern Ireland, at Stormont on 12 October and followed up with a letter on 18 October. After reporting briefly on the three earlier meetings, they proceeded to make the following points. First, through contact with the SDLP leaders they had become more sharply aware of the strength of feeling among Catholics against internment. Human rights – including the right to protest and the right of access to the due processes of the law including a fair trial – were now firmly on the world's agenda. Nationalists were more highly politicised than ever, and would simply not be satisfied with anything less than standards regarded as normal elsewhere. Second, allegations of brutality and torture against internees were a matter of grave concern to the deputation. The facts should be established and made known as quickly as possible. Early action was required in cases in which a tribunal recommended that internees be released. Third, both Mr Fitt and Mr Hume had indicated that they would become actively involved with other parties again if issues relating to internment could be resolved satisfactorily. Both, the deputation reported, had also stated their 'willingness to participate fully and constructively in public life in ... a reformed Northern Ireland State', so long as that reflected the will of the people. This seemed so important that the deputation wondered if the Prime Minister could use 'diplomatic or private channels' to confirm that it was indeed the case, so that he could then move things forward on as wide a front as possible. Fourth, the deputation welcomed Mr Faulkner's assurance that he intended to appoint a successor to Mr Bleakley as Minister of Community Relations, hopefully with increased powers. Fifth, although it was recognised that 'vigilante groups' were at present fulfilling a useful role in parts of Belfast, concern was expressed lest they were allowed to assume wider and longer-term responsibility for security matters. This, the deputation felt, could lead to dangerous and divisive developments. Sixth, the hope was expressed that members of the Cabinet could be persuaded to become more publicly identified with the government's reforming policies. Seventh, the importance of efforts by the Prime Minister 'to keep doors open for the minority' was emphasised:

> We believe that the present critical situation demands from leadership a high quality of statesmanship which rises far above mere party loyalty ... We believe it imperative that at all costs if public dialogue and conversation are impossible, every effort ought to be made to keep private channels open. Your power of initiative could be of tremendous value.

Eighth, the deputation sought permission to let it be known that their meeting had taken place as part of a series of interviews in which they had attempted to engage constructively with politicians in the critical community situation. Approaches were also made along these lines to the other three politicians with whom the deputation had met. All four agreed to 'go public' in this limited way, and a short factual statement was released giving the names of those involved in the conversations with an indication of the issues discussed.

One member of the deputation, David Poole, remembers the meeting with the N. I. Prime Minister as by far the least satisfying in the series (the series continued beyond my term as Organising Secretary). Poole's impression was that although Faulkner claimed to be willing to speak to anyone who would travel to Stormont to see him, it was only in that limited sense that his door was 'open'. He did not appear to be prepared to take the initiative in contacting political opponents. This was the background to the view expressed later by Poole in the ICC Executive in November 1971 that 'the Government of Northern Ireland (was) not interested in making contacts with the non-Unionist part of the community'.

Members of the deputation met the former British Prime Minister, Harold Wilson, who visited Northern Ireland in November. An invitation was also received through the General Secretary of the BCC from Nigel Spearing, a Labour MP, asking Irish church representatives to meet Labour and possibly Conservative backbenchers in London, in the hope of avoiding polarisation at Westminster on Northern Ireland affairs. The ICC Executive agreed to facilitate the sending of two Irish church representatives, one from an ICC member church and one from the RCC. Arrangements were left in my hands. It was made clear that those who went were not to speak on behalf of their churches or the Council, and that Conservative politicians should not be approached 'without reference to the leader of the Irish Unionist members', Robin (Sir Robin) Chichester-Clark, brother of the former N. I. Prime Minister. In the event I travelled to London alone, as in the time available I was not able to involve others. I met three Labour MPs, including Mr Spearing. In reporting back to the ICC Executive, I emphasised the importance of the Council and the Irish churches not neglecting the Westminster dimension in their response to the crisis in Northern Ireland. This became even more crucial following the suspension of the Stormont parliament in March 1972.

What of other developments following internment? On 26 September within sight of the end of the period for which he could serve, David Bleakley resigned as Minister of Community Relations in protest against internment and the government's failure to take new political initiatives. He was later to serve as Secretary of the ICC from 1980 to 1992. His successor as Minister of Community Relations was Basil McIvor, a barrister and Unionist MP with a Methodist background who later played a leading part in encouraging integrated education in the Province. G. B. Newe, a founder member of PACE and regional organiser and secretary to the N. I. Council of Social Service from 1948 to 1972, was also appointed Minister of State with cabinet rank by Faulkner, to help strengthen the work of community relations. Newe was the first Catholic to hold a ministerial position in the government of Northern Ireland, but before his six months of non-parliamentary ministerial life had been completed the Stormont government had been suspended. The Democratic Unionist Party, described as 'on the right on constitutional issues and on the left on social issues', was formed on 30 October, with Paisley its key figure. An IRA bomb exploded in the Post Office Tower in London on 31 October.

The Compton Report into allegations of brutality against detainees was published on 16 November. Methods of interrogation had included the 'five techniques', sleep deprivation, standing spreadeagled against a wall for long periods, placing a hood over the head, providing irregular and limited food and water, and the use of 'white noise' in the form of a constant humming sound. Compton's conclusion that individuals had not suffered physical brutality though there had been 'ill-treatment', left many people highly dissatisfied. Hayes, for example, later dismissed the report as 'shameful and infamous', with Compton attempting to make 'an entirely specious distinction between ill-treatment and torture'.[38] A three-man committee of British Privy Councillors reported on the findings the following February. One of them, Lord Gardiner (a former Labour Lord

Chancellor), was sharply critical, after which Heath announced that the interrogation techniques would no longer be used. On 4 December 1971 fifteen people were killed and thirteen injured when a loyalist bomb exploded at McGurk's bar in Belfast. The owner's wife and daughter were among the dead. On 12 December Jack Barnhill, a Unionist senator, was murdered at his home in Strabane. In all 22 people were killed within an eight day period in December.

What of church and other responses to the rapidly changing situation? I appealed to the residents of Greenisland in September to do all in their power to maintain good community relations, following reports that a petition had been circulated within the estate urging that no further houses be allocated to Roman Catholics. Those to whom I spoke said they had refused to sign the petition, which appeared to have originated outside Greenisland. 'We must maintain real contacts across the community', the *East Antrim Times* quoted me as saying. 'At all costs we must avoid unilateral action by one side or another', which was 'always inclined to back-fire.'[39]

A panel of church leaders from Ireland was given the opportunity to discuss the Northern Ireland situation at a session of the autumn meeting of the British Council of Churches at Dunblane, Scotland, from 26 to 27 October. The members of the panel were Archbishop George Simms, Dr Weir, Dr Gallagher and Bishop John Armstrong, with Arthur McArthur in the chair. The latter was General Secretary of the Presbyterian Church in England and convener of the BCC Advisory Group on Northern Ireland. A 'questions and comments' format was followed, to encourage discussion and to enable the latest developments to be taken into account. Robert Brown, an Irish member of the BCC and its Executive, reported on the session at the autumn meeting of the ICC in Belfast on 4 November. On the whole he had been disappointed. Many people in Britain still appeared to be unaware of crucial elements in the crisis, while British representatives found little in the session to give them hope. There did though appear to be general agreement that the army could not be withdrawn until terrorism was defeated. In the longer term Brown believed that a 'phased withdrawal' of the army was 'inevitable'. Three significant clusters of questions had emerged for

Irish churches and Christians. They would, he suspected, find them deeply disturbing. First, are Irish churches seriously considering the future of Northern Ireland either in a United Kingdom or an all-Ireland context? Second, is the Westminster form of democracy really suited to Northern Ireland, given its tendency to marginalise minorities? Are the churches willing to consider alternative patterns of democracy? Third, is the RCC being pressed to adopt the kind of religious, educational and social policies essential in a plural society? The meaning, nature and demands of democracy had to be examined in the light of the Christian faith, Brown urged.

Edward Rogers – General Secretary of the British Methodist Christian Citizenship Department, a former President of Conference and a prominent figure in both the BCC and the Free Church Federal Council in Britain – attended this meeting of Council. He pressed the question, can Northern Ireland and the Republic achieve stability so long as the island remains divided? Dean Charles Gray-Stack was concerned that the churches in Ireland increasingly appeared to be speaking with two voices, North and South. He feared that Protestant families in the Republic might be victimised due to divisions in the North. Dr Gallagher emphasised the need for people to be forward looking, seeking ways for Catholics and Protestants to live together. Barry Deane commented that integrated education should be considered in the South as well as the North. Two barriers to integration had already been removed in the South, he claimed, the Catholic ban on Catholic students attending Trinity College, Dublin, and the Gaelic Athletic Association's ban on 'foreign games'. ICC member churches should reject the Irish government proposals for 'community' (mainly Catholic) schools and 'comprehensive' (mainly Protestant) schools, he argued. Dr Weir felt that as church representatives they should not 'play at politics', but should give priority to proclaiming the gospel. Dr Gallagher endorsed a comment by Edward Rogers, that churches need not be amateurish in their approach to political questions and politicians. Member churches, he continued, made it difficult for the ICC to adopt a more professional approach by refusing to relinquish their independence. This prevented a more realistic sharing of resources, including personnel. Canon Elliott agreed, and pressed the churches to show greater willingness to study and respond to issues together. The Irish government needed to be made more aware of Northern Protestant fears.

On 13 November 1971 the churches' correspondent in the *Belfast Telegraph* placed these comments and those, as noted, by Robert Brown and others alongside those of Bishop Cahal Daly (later Cardinal) as expressed in London on 10 November, suggesting that they revealed 'a surprising amount of common ground'. As an Ulsterman who had previously served for twenty-five years on the staff at Queen's University, Belfast, and who was now Bishop of Ardagh and Clonmacnoise in the South, Bishop Daly felt able to pay tribute to 'the Protestant and Presbyterian tradition' in the North and the community's capacity to create 'genuinely democratic institutions' within Northern Ireland. Arguably the problem in the North was not so much that the institutions were not democratic but that in a divided society they did not operate democratically. Like other leaders at the time in the ICC, the article in the *Belfast Telegraph* suggested, Daly saw the way forward in terms of the introduction of 'political measures of a radical nature … assuring the minority of a share, as of right, in political responsibility and decision-making power.'

On 3 December the BCC Executive Committee issued a statement on Northern Ireland in which it claimed that the Christian faith required of its disciples 'a loyalty wide and deep enough to transcend the traditional divisions between Catholics and Protestants.' After paying tribute to those – both Catholics and Protestants – who exercised restraint, the Committee called for 'still greater efforts' to establish 'effective co-operative ventures':

> Aware that such initiatives may have divisive effects within the Churches … it believes that Christian duty requires that new efforts be made to re-establish and deepen that fellowship across the denominational divisions which has been so gravely injured in the past two years.

The BCC's Advisory Group, established late in 1969 with the task of maintaining liaison with the ICC and providing guidance to the BCC in matters relating mainly to the North, considered 'the serious issues raised by the economic situation, escalating violence, internment and the Compton Report.'

The Council's most ambitious initiative in terms of wider education and communication was jointly promoted with the Conference of European Churches (CEC) and took place in December. Dr Glen Williams, General Secretary of CEC, had visited Northern Ireland in September 1971 following correspondence the previous year. The visit led to two important developments which helped to forge closer links between the churches in Europe and Ireland, and enabled European churches to become more aware of the community crisis in Ireland. First, Dr Schilling, the Deputy Editor-in-Chief of the German EPD Evangelical Church Press Service (a resource also used by other European countries and churches), spent over two weeks in Ireland in November. He was especially interested in church programmes, Catholic and Protestant, in response to the Troubles and ways in which the churches were being affected by the crisis. The visit enabled him to pass on valuable information and material to other European church-related agencies and journals. Second, from 2 to 4 December an information seminar on the Troubles and the churches, organised by the ICC and attended by forty church-related representatives from ten European countries – most of them with media reponsibilities – was held in the Edenmore Hotel, Whiteabbey, near Belfast. As part of the programme, visits were arranged to troubled areas in and around Belfast. Archbishop Simms, as ICC Chairman, presided over the seminar. Speakers included Padraig Murphy of Corpus Christi church, Ballymurphy, Alf McCreary (journalist), Robin Bailie (the Newtownabbey MP and Stormont Minister of Commerce), Dr Gallagher and David Bleakley. The seminar had a dual purpose, to encourage the Irish churches through the presence of church representatives from Europe, and to give people from Europe an overview of the Troubles. Topics included the historical background, political attitudes, the Orange Order, the minority's attitudes towards Northern Ireland, community relations, and the position of the churches.

One of the most striking addresses was by Padraig Murphy, who, in addition to stressing the need for reform and the abandonment of oppression, argued forceably that the murder of soldiers, police and ordinary civilians 'could not be condoned or accepted by anyone who professed to be a human being let alone a Christian'. Dr Gallagher also received headlines for his claim that the IRA and the Protestant right wing were at one in opposing closer involvement with Europe, since this 'would make a narrow and prejudiced nationalism outdated'.

I sent an open letter, later published and endorsed by the ICC Executive, to two MPs who had been invited to the seminar but did not attend. Gerry Fitt did not reply to the invitation, and Ian Paisley refused to attend because of the initiative's ecumenical nature. By failing to attend or to send representatives, I claimed, they had let their parties down and those who had elected them.[40] Many people spoke of the value of the seminar. Personal contacts were made which continued to grow and bear fruit through the 70s. Community projects in Northern Ireland bene-fitted from increased support, and two accounts of the seminar were published in Germany.

January to July 1972
The sickening sequence of violent events gathered pace through 1972. All parades – Catholic and Protestant, Nationalist and Unionist – had been banned since August 1971, a ban which was renewed in the new year to lessen the chances of further sectarian conflict. On 30 January, following an unlawful civil rights march and rally attended by nearly 10,000 people on what became known as 'Bloody Sunday', thirteen men, all apparently un-armed, were shot dead and seventeen others were wounded by the Parachute Regiment in Derry. For Nationalists, the day was summed up by a coroner who described the killings as 'sheer unadulterated bloody murder'.[41] Cabinet papers for 1972, re-leased under the thirty year rule, suggest that even before Bloody Sunday Catholic alienation was at an 'unparalleled' and increasing level. Inevitably things deteriorated rapidly through-out Ireland following Bloody Sunday. A national day of mourn-ing was declared in the Republic, the Irish ambassador was re-called from London, and 'the intensity of anti-British feeling (in Dublin) was potent with danger'.[42] Following church services for the victims, protests and demonstrations, the British em-bassy in Dublin was burned down on 2 February. In the North the former N. I. Minister of Home Affairs, William Craig, launched Ulster Vanguard on 9 February, an umbrella organis-

ation for right wing Unionists. 'If and when the politicians fail us', he declared ominously at a rally attended by 60,000 people, 'it may be our job to liquidate the enemy.' On 25 February John Taylor, the Stormont Minister for Home Affairs, sustained serious gunshot wounds from an Official IRA attempt on his life. On 20 March six people were killed and more than a hundred injured when a Provisional IRA car bomb exploded without warning in Belfast. By then Edward Heath had come to the conclusion that Faulkner's government could not deliver either security or political stability. When the UUP refused to hand over law and order powers to London, the British Prime Minister announced Stormont's suspension. The N. I. parliament met for the last time on 28 March, 'prorogued' initially for twelve months but effectively abolished in the form in which it had been familiarly known. Direct rule, administered through a newly created government department – the Northern Ireland Office (NIO) – was to remain in place for many years, with no prospect of an old style Unionist government returning. It was the realisation of Unionism's worst fears and a step broadly welcomed by others, though Republicans and Nationalists viewed with mixed feelings the strengthening of Westminster's position within Northern Ireland. The Irish government formally welcomed the suspension of Stormont, and re-established diplomatic relations with Britain.

The worst day of violence in the weeks immediately following the introduction of direct rule came on 14 April, with twenty-three explosions in different parts of Northern Ireland. On 18 April the Widgery Report on Bloody Sunday was published. Dismissed by Nationalists as a 'whitewash' and a cover-up, it claimed that those organising the illegal march had created 'a highly dangerous situation in which a clash ... was almost inevitable'. It also acknowledged that the firing from some soldiers bordered 'on the reckless' and that 'none of the deceased or wounded was proved to have been shot holding a firearm or bomb'. Widgery's crucial reliance on the accounts of soldiers, though they differed considerably from those given on the day itself, raise serious questions about the Report's findings. A recent study of the IRA concludes that 'the weight of evidence suggests that the killings of Bloody Sunday were utterly unjustified.'[43] Eight people were killed on 21 May in gunfire between the (Catholic) Ballymurphy and the neighbouring (Protestant) Springmartin estates in Belfast. On 25 May the Official IRA in Derry kidnapped and killed William Best, a nineteen-year-old soldier home on leave in the city to visit his family. Opinion across the community was outraged, with four hundred mothers marching on the Official Sinn Féin offices and launching a verbal attack on those inside. The SDLP called upon Nationalists who had been boycotting public offices, to end their protest. Four days later the Official IRA called a halt to its military campaign. The Provisional IRA opposed the killing of William Best, but announced that its own military campaign would continue. In Libya, Colonel Gaddafi declared on 11 June that he had supplied arms to 'the Irish revolutionaries', indirectly drawing attention to the internationalisation of the Troubles. On 14 June John Hume and Paddy Devlin of the SDLP met the Provisional leadership in Derry, with the IRA outlining its conditions for talks with the British. These included the granting of political status to republican prisoners, an independent witness to be present at discussions, the meeting to be held at a location other than Stormont, and the Provisionals to be allowed to choose their own team. These conditions were passed on to William Whitelaw (the N. I. Secretary of State) who regarded them as 'fairly innocuous', and accepted them. The after-effects of the decision to grant political status were long lasting, providing the background to a highly divisive hunger strike in 1981. Recent revelations under the thirty year rule indicate that Gerry Adams and David O'Connell of the Provisional IRA secretly met two senior NIO officials for exploratory talks on 20 June 1972 at Ballyarnett, a 'safe house' on the Derry side of the Donegal border. This in turn led the Provisional IRA to suspend its military operations from 26 June, to prepare for talks with the British. William Whitelaw and other British ministers met six members of the Provisional IRA for what proved to be unproductive talks in London on 7 July. On 13 July the Provisional IRA ended its two week ceasefire, and the following day four civilians and a soldier were killed. On 21 July, commonly referred to as 'Bloody Friday', the IRA set off twenty-six bombs in Belfast, killing 11 people and injuring 130. On 31 July, following these atrocities and the failure of talks, the British authorities gave the order for twelve thousand soldiers with bulldozers and tanks (stripped of their guns) to smash their way into 'no-go' areas in Belfast and Derry, to restore government control. Three IRA car bombs exploded in Claudy on 31 July, killing eight people, Protestant and Catholic neighbours. Official papers recently released have reopened the question, rumoured at the time, as to whether Jim Chesney, a local Catholic priest, was directly involved as an IRA activist in the Claudy bombing. In all, more than 650 people died in Northern Ireland as a result of violence between August 1971 and the end of 1972, by far the worst phase in the Troubles.

The sharp increase in violence in 1972 presented a major challenge to the churches and to people of all backgrounds and shades of opinion. On 7 January I publicly invited Desmond Wilson to clarify a statement attributed to him in an interview reported in the *Belfast Telegraph* under the heading 'Violence could be only way – Priest'. We knew each other, and had for example shared a platform at a large ecumenical gathering in Carlow. In this case I sought to encourage a public debate on violence. Wilson, who would not have claimed that his views were typical of those of other priests and which ran counter to the statements of the Irish Catholic bishops on violence, replied that repeated condemnations did little good and could do harm; that the vast majority of Christians in the wider world clearly believed that the use of force was justifiable in some circumstances; that only those who could demonstrate how justice could be achieved by non-violent means earned the right to condemn violence; and that he himself personally detested violence. 'There are', he added, 'so many kinds of injustice, some of them extremely refined, that I wonder if we have any right to hope that counter-violence can be staved off indefinitely.'[44] The correspondence misfired in the opinion of one person, who in an unsigned letter claimed to represent the view of 'A Church of Ireland Protestant' and dismissed me as 'a hypocrite sunk in depravity'. The letter concluded with a prayer that the Lord would frustrate all ecumenical endeavour!

On 23 January at an ecumenical service in Donegall Square Methodist church – my 'home church' before entering the ministry, now an Ulster bank in Belfast's city centre – I was the preacher with Catholic and Protestant leaders taking part. After referring to a cacophany of voices, contradictory and confusing, all demanding to be heard, I continued:

> There was the shrill voice of sectarian hate; ominous mutter-ings calling for revenge and reprisals; the broken sobs of parents and children mourning their dead; anxious calls for forgiveness, restraint and co-operation; sullen threats; bitter accusations; wild, incoherent, uncontrolled utterances ... But above all and despite all (was) heard the quiet, persuasive, urgent voice of Jesus that refused to be silenced, 'I command you to love one another.' Jesus' love leaps over barriers and refuses to be hemmed in or restricted in any way. Our (love) must be like that too, generous and catholic, reaching out to-wards all.

Jesus' love was practical, not sentimental. It was relevant to the needs of those he met. Love of neighbour compels us also to face hard issues. For example, what form should love of neighbour take when feelings run high in an area and our neighbour is being intimidated to leave his home, or when the breadwinner in a family has been interned, or when the life of a Catholic member of the police has been threatened? Jesus' love was not simply individual and personal. It sought to challenge struc-tures and to create community. Neighbourly love had to inform public attitudes and policies, attempting to build a society marked by justice, mercy and peace:

> In deciding where factories and other facilities will be located; what methods are to be used to advance his political and other aims, and what those aims are; and how to put down violence and restore order, (a person) will be guided by a de-sire to give expression to Christian love and concern. He can never abandon in public life the principles by which he seeks to live in private life.[45]

This service too drew criticism. A letter claimed to be from 'a former member of Greenisland church', who now followed Paisley. 'Paisley', commented the writer, 'preaches the old time religion, not a gutless, ecumenical, "be ye reconciled one to an-other" religion.'[46]

I returned to the related themes of violence and community disorder in a sermon in Greenisland on 6 February, entitled

'Christian Responsibility with regard to Terrorism'. The sermon attracted considerable media attention. There was, I argued, a need to establish broad principles on which both Catholics and Protestants agreed. Violent acts were not the sole preserve of 'terrorists':

> 'Terrorists' are not the only people capable of engaging in terrorist activity. Even in a civilised society ... the institutions of the state are capable of resorting at least to isolated acts of terrorism. Terrorism is a fact of life in Northern Ireland today ... Every bomb thrown, every shot fired, contributes to an already intolerable burden of grief, agony and loss ... (of which) the brutal and damaging effects extend far beyond those directly involved.

Terrorism, I continued, threatened the economy, placed additional strain on community relations and undermined the moral well-being of society. It appealed particularly to vulnerable young people, falsely appearing to offer an alternative to poverty and powerlessness. We differ as political parties, churches and organisations on various issues, perhaps even in our definition of a just society. We ought however to unite in opposing unlawful force, using only just means to pursue our goals. Lumping all Roman Catholics with the IRA is totally irresponsible, as is taking part in illegal processions or joining illegal organisations to defeat the IRA, I declared. Institutions of the state must resist any tendency to become brutal and oppressive. If the police and army are accused of oppression, the facts must be clearly established and those accused brought quickly to court. We must pray for a radical change in people's hearts and attitudes. All need to be lifted above narrow sectarian and selfish concerns until the desire to know and do God's will becomes our chief concern.[47]

For Good Friday, the Presbyterian Moderator, the Methodist President, and the two Archbishops of Armagh, issued a joint appeal in which they spoke of the need for repentance for the 'failure to live out the Christian message of reconciliation':

> So many of us have mistaken patriotism for piety, forgetting that devotion to our country doesn't mean revulsion from each other. A nation's best defenders are not the men of bitterness and violence, but (those) who are prepared to accept

the teaching of Christ and demonstrate it as a way of life ... Our prayer is that from our splintered society will come a strength of purpose to all people ...; and that the Christian Church will become more and more a channel of outreach rather than a citadel of self-defence ... Our service of God becomes counterfeit if it does not involve our reaching across the street, across the social and religious divisions, across the political divisions of our society.

About the same time the ICC received a gift from the Dean and Chapter of St Paul's Cathedral, Calcutta. A cross of charred wood from Bangladesh, it continued the central theme of the crucified Christ as our healer and the radical challenge of costly Christian discipleship.

On March 29 the ICC Executive issued a statement which responded to the suspension of the Stormont parliament. Against a background of growing anger within the majority community, the Executive appealed for constructive and positive co-operation with Westminster especially during the initial period of twelve months for which Stormont had been suspended:

At this time of crisis, we call upon all in our member churches to commend their faith by the quality of their lives, to uphold lawful authority, to maintain the peace and to seek the reconciliation of our divided community. We understand the strong feeling of shock and the reaction produced by the announcement of the Westminster government. We nevertheless declare ourselves totally opposed to any type of political action which must inevitably lead to intimidation, a heightening of community tension and further threats to the economic survival of the country ... (There is a) paramount necessity for finding a solution to the Northern Ireland problem acceptable to the majority in all sections of the community. No solution can be reached on terms acceptable to one side only. What is at stake in Ireland is the well-being of all its people – their future, safety, health and livelihood, the things which make the full life possible. We re-affirm our conviction that as Churches we must strive for a society free from fear and want, free to choose a way of life acceptable to all its people, in which all will be free to worship God in accordance with their conscience. We are called to courageous, costly and possibly unpopular action on behalf of all ... The well-being and future of Northern Ireland are the responsibility of all its political parties. They (must) use the coming twelve months as an opportunity to act constructively with the government of the United Kingdom in an attempt to create a society in which men of violence no longer hold sway, and in which the will of the political majority (both Protestants and Roman Catholics) is clearly established.

This statement received wide coverage. It was for example quoted at length in the *Irish Times*,[48] and was the reference point for much of the discussion at the ICC meeting in Dublin on 13 April. As we shall see, it was referred to again in a different context at the end of June.

The debate on the role of the churches at the April meeting of the Council was lively. Barry Deane commented that he could not see a way forward except in the context of a united Ireland, whether in 'a republic, a monarchy, a condominium or in some other form'. Whatever form it took, the question had to be faced. Dr Kenneth Milne, the C of I's Education Secretary and an observer at the Council, commented that at times the Council's statements appeared 'to have the citizens of Sandy Row much more in mind than the citizens of the Falls Road'. 'Northern Nationalists', he continued, 'had a deep cultural and psychological commitment to Irish nationalism.' They were not just being 'difficult and militant'. It was 'bred in people's bones', and the churches as all-Ireland bodies needed to be more sensitive to the issue. John Radcliffe of the Non-Subscribing Presbyterian Church and Vice-Chairman of the Council, emphasised the need for consensus politics. It was not so much the ICC's job to pronounce on political strategies and solutions as to clarify moral issues, commented Dr Gallagher:

> One thing the SDLP, the IRA and the NICRA have done is to show that unilateral government is not possible, but equally government is not possible without the consent of the majority. We must find a way of government by consent ... Violence had reduced the number of jobs as well as turning children into criminals.

Dr Weir questioned the right of the Council to speak on political matters, but I reminded members of the breadth of the Council's

constitution when it spoke of the member churches and communions joining 'in united effort to promote the physical, moral
and social welfare of the people, and the extension of the rule of
Christ among all nations and over every region of human life'.
This, I argued, gave the Council authority to address political issues. The Executive's statement of 29 March was endorsed by
the Council.[49]

A remark by the Cardinal in response to direct rule came in
for criticism, when he said in an interview in Dublin that he
looked for an end to IRA violence and hoped that progress could
eventually be made towards a united Ireland 'by peaceful mutual
agreement.' This comment, according to Gallagher and Worrall
in *Christians in Ulster 1968-1980,* 'was scarcely calculated to allay
Protestant fears'.[50] Yet, as already noted, unity by consent had
been raised as a possibility by an ICC deputation in conversation with the Taoiseach in August the previous year. Unity by
consent was referred to again, as we have seen, in the meeting of
the full Council in the presence of the press only days after the
Cardinal had spoken. As Deane was quoted in the *Irish Times* as
saying, unity was 'not a matter that could be swept under the
carpet'.

The Executive Committee had earlier expressed concern
about the future of the N. I. Community Relations Commission
following Dr Hayes' resignation and disparaging remarks by
John Taylor concerning him. A message had been sent from the
Executive conveying appreciation for Hayes' work with the
Commission. He was invited to address the Spring meeting of
the Council on the task of community reconstruction, a significant initiative by the Council in view of the controversy surrounding his departure from the Commission. Hayes emphasised the special role of the churches in drawing alongside people
in their fears, commending non-violent ways of resolving conflict, and encouraging cross-community contact. 'The first people the churches had to bring together were the church leaders
… and their clergy at various levels', he suggested. The divisions in the North – whether social, sectarian or communal –
were anti-Christian he said, and the churches had greater responsibility than any other sector in seeking to resolve them. He
would like to see more devolution in society, with for example

wardens appointed in housing estates. In response to a question, he declared himself in favour of integrated education. Denominational education was 'not the root of all our problems', but it did reinforce division and encouraged an 'us' and 'them' mentality, he argued. Integrated education could be an important element in the liberalisation of society as a whole.[51]

At an Executive Committee meeting, also held on 13 April, I reported that on behalf of the Council I had contacted William Whitelaw, who had suggested a meeting with Lord Windlesham, a minister in the N. I. Office. Members of the deputation who had earlier been in touch with politicians met Lord Windlesham, and drew his attention to initiatives and statements by the ICC on social, political and community issues. They also informed him of the Council's contacts with the RCC. The deputation pressed the importance of economic and social issues, including jobs and houses, and emphasised that the police should take steps to make themselves more acceptable across the community. Hope was expressed that government ministers would present a high visibility within the Province, and that the administration would seek to keep ahead of developments in a dynamic and rapidly changing situation.

In a sermon in Greenisland on 28 May, I welcomed the courageous words and witness of the four hundred mothers who had marched on the Sinn Féin offices in Derry to launch a verbal attack on those who had killed the teenage soldier, William Best:

This past week … there was the usual catalogue of catastrophes, callously planned to bring ever closer the day of uncontrolled sectarian violence. More lives were taken, more homes invaded … more buildings destroyed. But other things happened as well, new things that we have been praying for months would happen … I refer of course to the stand that has been taken on the side of the cessation of violence in the Creggan and the Bogside … We have been disappointed before and may be again, but let us record such actions and words as encouraging signs … Somebody asked me the other day what I thought of the women of Derry following their demonstration for peace. I simply replied that I hope and pray. (That) is what we all need to do, to hope and pray that strength may be given to such people to maintain a strong

moral stand against all forms of demoralising violence, and
that God's grace may be given in the struggle for peace based
on justice.[52]

At my final ICC Executive Committee meeting on 30 June, a discussion took place in response to a letter from Wilbert Forker. A
minister of the MCI and at the time *Chef de Press* in the communi-
cations department of the WCC, Forker had written that some
statements by the Irish churches had given the impression to
people outside Ireland that the Irish churches were divided,
North and South. Bandmaster Webster of the Savation Army
agreed, and referred to the statement of 29 March as in part im-
plying a church in Ireland divided between two jurisdictions. Dr
Jack Weir disagreed, claiming that the Executive would have
been 'highly irresponsible' had it expressed itself in any other
terms. As already noted, the issue of the churches needing to reflect their all-Ireland identity had arisen even more sharply in
September 1971 following the introduction of internment.

Little has been said about the churches' youth scene during
the Troubles. The main vehicle for ecumenical youth work and
communication was the Youth Committee of Irish Churches
(YCIC) of the ICC. Described in the mid 60s as 'little more than a
talking shop' and 'rather toothless',[53] things were soon to
change with full-time youth officers of the ICC's larger member
churches coming to the fore in attempts to respond to the fast deteriorating situation within the community. These were Gordon
Gray of the PCI, Cecil Hyland of the C of I, and John Knox of the
MCI (who succeeded Charles Eyre in 1969). Others were involved with them including Robin Eames, who was to become
Bishop of Derry and Archbishop of Armagh, and Geoffrey
Corry who was later associated with Glencree (a centre in county Wicklow committed to promoting cross-community relations). YCIC facilitated an annual Irish Christian Youth
Assembly (ICYA), of which further mention will be made in the
next chapter. Although the official theme of the ICYA event held
in Belfast in 1969 was the Christian use of Sunday, civil rights
understandably emerged as a key issue.

The three BCC member churches in Ireland – the C of I, the
MCI and the PCI – participated in the Youth Department of the
BCC, with Dr Samuel (later bishop) Poyntz the department's

chairman from the mid to late 1960s. The Irish churches also began to play a greater part in the European and world ecumenical youth scene. For example, every year a full-time youth officer attended the European regional church youth leaders' conference, initially organised by the WCC Youth Department, with each youth officer taking it in turn to represent the others. It was however decided that Europe, like other regions, should have its own ecumenical youth structure. In 1969 the Ecumenical Youth Council for Europe (EYCE) was formed, which took over responsibility for European regional youth conferences. EYCE's founding chairman was Dublin-born and Cambridge-educated Foster Murphy. A member of the C of I, he had formerly been SCM secretary for Ireland and secretary of YCIC, and was by this time secretary of the Youth Department of the BCC. Piet Bouman of EYCE visited Ireland in 1970, and was invited to address the ICC on 9 March. He identified EYCE's three main concerns as economic justice, East/West contacts and relations with the Roman Catholic and Eastern Orthodox Churches.

In 1969, in addition to their co-operation through YCIC, the church youth officers began to meet informally once a month in each other's homes, to share information, to discuss their work and to encourage wider participation in events. Their agenda included prayer, Bible study, sharing problems and concerns, and jointly planning courses and seminars. By 1972 they had become a virtual 'team ministry' in areas of their work, and been joined by Sean McCartney and Colm Campbell, two Catholic priests, the latter being the youth officer of the RC diocese of Down and Connor. Major Albert Wall of the Salvation Army and Peter Quigley also became involved, the latter in a personal capacity though he was the Baptist youth officer. Representation and roles at events and within youth structures were worked out on these occasions. Work began on a youth leaders' manual, *Together with Youth*, for use within the ICC member churches, prompted in part by a publication in the Church of Scotland.

As growing numbers of young people were caught up in illegal organisations and street violence, the youth officers attempted to present attractive and challenging alternative programmes. A visit by Gordon Gray and Cecil Hyland to the Falls

Road at the height of the rioting in mid August 1969, re-enforced their sense of the need to take fresh initiatives. A major break-through was achieved when, following careful planning, a joint Catholic/Protestant adventure youth camp took place at the Presbyterian site at Guysmere, Castlerock, in August 1970. Almost a hundred teenage boys from Belfast's Shankill and Falls roads participated. The army youth team, part of a 'hearts and minds' initiative, organised adventure activities such as canoe-ing, abseiling and orienteering. Student volunteers from other countries, recruited through the WCC, added an international dimension. The overall leadership was provided by the youth officers including two Catholic priests. The youth camp was re-peated in 1971 with young people recruited from a wider area, and in 1972 a camp was held in the Isle of Man, partly funded by money raised through a public appeal by an Isle of Man news-paper. In 1971 an ecumenical youth vigil was held on St Patrick's night at Stranmillis College, Belfast, led by Michel Quoist, a French Catholic priest and author of *Prayers of Life*, when around 400 Catholic and Protestant young adults spent the night focus-ing on issues of justice and peace.

On 11 June I read a statement at the end of an evening service in Greenisland church, and released it to the media. It stated that I was opposed to the growing practice of the Ulster Defence Association (UDA), the largest Protestant paramilitary organis-ation, in imposing token 'no-go' areas. Whilst appreciating the frustration of peace-loving citizens – Protestants and Catholics – at continuing violence, I was against the action for two reasons. First, though initiated in the name of Protestantism and presented as a protest against long-standing republican 'no-go' areas, they disrupted life in many districts including some which had previ-ously been trouble-free. This restricted the freedom of people, even preventing some from attending the church of their choice, and was 'offensive to Christian conscience'. Second, though set up in the name of law and order, they were 'self-defeating', im-posing additional burdens on the police and army, bringing hooligan elements to the fore, and throwing the minority into the arms of the IRA at a time when some were distancing them-selves from republican paramilitaries:

All decent citizens have a right, even a duty, to be concerned

> about ending violence and restoring peace, but this will
> never be done by one section of the community acting unilat-
> erally against another or against properly constituted author-
> ity. Such action, however well intentioned, only serves to
> heighten fear and tension further, and propels us in the di-
> rection of even more tragic civil strife and economic ruin …
> Our very survival demands that moderate people should
> speak and act together, and in this connection … Christians,
> both Protestants and Roman Catholics, have a particular re-
> sponsibility to set the pace by practising love, forgiveness
> and trust … Others may maintain a discreet silence … I can-
> not, even though I realise that I shall forfeit popularity and
> may even put my safety at risk … Obedience to my con-
> science and to my understanding of the gospel requires that I
> speak in this way at this time.

Nothing I said or did in my entire ministry attracted as much
media attention or public response.[54] Reference to the statement
was carried in radio and TV news bulletins and in the news-
papers. Many phone calls – some anonymous, abusive and
threatening, others supportive – were received. The first was
from a person claiming to be 'C of I' and a Councillor. He was
strongly opposed to the statement on the grounds that he believed there had been inadequate political leadership and protection in Northern Ireland for three years. The second was from
Harold Sloan, who became the President of the Methodist
Church the following year, to say that he had received a threat to
burn down Greenisland church. A woman rang from Mossley,
to say she was a member of the Church of God and was against
the statement. She felt that the UDA was doing a good job. A
woman rang from Stranmillis. She too was opposed and mis-
trusted all peace moves by Roman Catholics. Two Presbyterian
women rang to express support. They were unhappy with their
own church's lead, they said. A man claiming to be 'the chairman of the UDA' rang to say that the statement 'would not be
taken lying down'. Asked if this was meant as a threat, he rang
off. Monsignor Ryan phoned to say that the statement made him
'immensely proud and grateful'. Dill Henderson, Secretary of
the Community Relations Commission, rang to say she 'could
have cheered' on hearing the statement. The wife of a senior

serving army officer in Derry, herself a Catholic, phoned. Her car had been highjacked seven times. She despaired of the lead being given by the RCC, and hoped that Wesminster would allow the army to enter the Bogside. Anne Dickson, the local MP, phoned in support, as did a member of the Bahai community, an Alliance party member, and Billy Blease (later Lord Blease) on behalf of the Trade Union movement. A senior church figure rang to warn that I was on my own. The wife of Bishop Richard Hanson (Anthony Hanson's twin brother), Mary, sent a letter of support. Another person wrote anonymously, signing as 'Non Communist' and 'in disgust'. This letter accused me of fraternising with communists, and cautioned that I 'might be a marked man ... not by (my) enemy the Protestants, but by the very men' with whom I sympathised. I should discard my communist cloak, and recognise that Christ was 'still on the throne'. A judgement day was coming, and I should beware.

Twenty-four hours after making the statement I had to leave Greenisland to attend the annual Methodist Conference, held that year in Dublin. I left my wife at home with our four children, to cope with the continuing flak and danger. Neighbours and others were however at hand, if needed, to give support and encouragement. At the annual Methodist Conference no mention was made of my service with the ICC, though my 'pioneering' work for world development was noted and good wishes were extended on my new appointment with the Methodist Missionary Society (MMS), London. Was this a further indication that ecumenical work was not accepted as within the mainstream of the MCI's work?

I travelled with my family to London in the summer, to work at the headquarters of the MMS in Marylebone Road. My job was essentially to co-ordinate the work of a sizeable team of people responsible for world mission education within Methodism. My engagement with the churches in Ireland had been intense and unrelenting, and proved difficult to shake off. To a degree the past pursued me. For example, I found myself engaged in a painful controversy in the pages of the *Methodist Recorder* after a call by the Rev Dr the Lord Soper, the renowned broadcaster, pacifist, former President of the Methodist Conference and open-air speaker. Dr Soper had encouraged people in Britain 'to atone for the military action on Bloody Sunday' by travelling to Derry in large numbers to take part in a vigil to commemorate the deaths on the first anniversary of the event. Soper's call – contained in a letter to the *Recorder* – led to a storm of protest from people who feared that the vigil might prove disruptive and divisive.[55] Despite receiving a warm welcome from new colleagues, I initially suffered from a level of culture shock as a Northern Irishman in London. Graffiti near our home was unsettling, 'Blacks and Irish, go home!' Both categories applied to us as a family.

CHAPTER 3

The ICC and the Roman Catholic Church

AN OVERVIEW OF ATTITUDES AND RELATIONSHIPS
BEFORE THE SECOND VATICAN COUNCIL

How did Protestants and Roman Catholics think of, and relate to, one another in the 1950s and 1960s? What contacts did their churches make? Were things different after the Second Vatican Council? How did the Troubles influence matters? Did the Irish Council of Churches have a role in encouraging change? At a personal level, especially in rural areas, Protestant and Catholic neighbours often got on well together and supported one another through difficult times. In noting the lack of any formal contact between the Roman Catholic Church and the ICC and the Protestant churches before the Troubles, we need to remember that this was not unusual on the world scene at that time. Things were to change following the Second Vatican Council and the Uppsala assembly of the WCC. Until they did and there was greater contact between the RCC and the Council, the title – the Irish Council of Churches – was something of a misnomer.

Generalisations by Michael Hurley, the Jesuit scholar and ecumenist, about Irish inter-church attitudes and relations ring true, that anti-Romanism was an entrenched feature of Irish Protestantism, anti-Protestantism was a marked feature of Irish Catholicism, and each 'side' was content with its isolationism.[1] There was, too, an accompanying attitude of each regarding the other with conversionist zeal. Prior to the Vatican Council the RCC still viewed the 'non-Catholic' churches in terms of the uncompromising words of the 1928 encyclical letter of Pius XI, *Mortalium Animos:*

> There is but one way in which the unity of Christians may be fostered, and that is by furthering the return to the one true Church of Christ of those who are separated from it; for from that one true Church they have in the past fallen away.[2]

If Rome thought of unity with non-Catholics only in terms of their 'return' to the Catholic fold, Protestants envisaged closer relations with Catholics only on the basis of them turning their backs on Romanism and embracing the Reformation faith. For many on both sides there was no room for half measures.

Hurley also draws attention to the fact that it was not simply a matter of isolationism and conversionist zeal between Catholics and Protestants. Denominationalism was deep-seated within and between the Protestant churches, the main denominations being strong enough to live to themselves, little interested in co-operation with one another. 'For the most part ... we were indifferent to to ecumenism', writes Hurley. 'The churches had no felt need of each other. We all felt self-sufficient.'[3]

Significant and related developments within Protestantism encouraged a new emphasis and approach. In late September 1963 the United Council of Churches and Religious Communions in Ireland (UCCI) – it became known as the Irish Council of Churches in 1965 – held a conference in Greystones, county Wicklow. This conference recommended that those attending it should try to make the UCCI 'a more effective instrument of common action', and consider how they could respond 'in truth and love' to those Catholics who expressed a sense of fellowship towards them. This encouraged individuals in the Protestant churches to engage in dialogue with Catholics, for example in the annual ecumenical conferences which began in 1964 at Glenstal, a Benedictine abbey in county Limerick, and from 1966 at Greenhills, Drogheda. The Greystones conference also prompted the Presbyterian Inter-Church Relations Committee to draw up a statement on relations between Presbyterians and Catholics. This was generally well received and led the General Assembly to approve a resolution in 1965 which encouraged Presbyterians to acknowledge, and ask forgiveness for, attitudes and actions towards Catholics considered unworthy of followers of Jesus Christ. The Assembly called on Presbyterians 'to deal with all conflicts of interests, loyalties and beliefs' in a spirit of love and in accordance with scriptural teaching rather than suspicion and intolerance. Carlisle Patterson, who proposed the resolution at the Presbyterian General Assembly, had been part-time Organising Secretary of the UCCI from 1958 to 1962.

CHANGE AND 'NO CHANGE'
FOLLOWING THE SECOND VATICAN COUNCIL

The second Vatican Council signalled a more positive attitude towards ecumenism among Catholics worldwide. Phrases in the Decree on Ecumenism such as 'separated brethren' as an alternative way of referring to 'non-Catholics'; the acknowledgement that 'often enough (people) of both sides were to blame' when divisions occurred; the church's need for 'continual reformation' as it goes its 'pilgrim way'; and the emphasis on 'spiritual ecumenism' involving changes of 'heart and holiness of life' among the faithful, all promised hope of fundamental change within the RCC and greatly enhanced prospects of closer relationships. Not surprisingly, however, progress in Ireland was to take time with some of the early signs being far from encouraging. When for example John Charles McQuaid, the Catholic Archbishop of Dublin, returned from the Vatican Council and preached in the Pro-Cathedral, he sought to comfort and encourage those who felt threatened:

> Now is our work completed ... One could not but feel that God the Holy Ghost had guided our deliberations. You may have been worried by much talk of changes to come. Allow me to reassure you. No change will worry the tranquillity of your Christian lives.[4]

Even five years later, when a new structure was proposed for the ICC-related Irish Christian Youth Assembly (ICYA) – to make it a forum open to Irish young people irrespective of denomination, with its steering committee given freedom to plan the annual Assembly – the Archbishop remained cautious. Geoffrey Corry, a young Methodist layman, had invited RC Bishop-elect Eamonn Casey to address the ICYA in 1971, in recognition of his work on housing with the organisation Shelter. Archbishop McQuaid advised Casey to turn the invitation down:

> The Irish Christian Youth Assembly is not known to us Catholics here and the new venture, which hopes to embrace Catholic youth, has some worrying aspects. It is liable to intensify an existing confusion.[5]

One wonders what 'worrying aspects' McQuaid perceived at the time. What 'existing confusion' had he in mind, and what seemed likely to add to it? Were Catholic youth groups already meeting with Protestant young adults, to explore issues of faith in a changing society? Were difficult and disturbing questions arising? Was there a fear, for example, that closer contact between Catholic and Protestant young people might push into prominence such thorny questions as inter-communion and inter-church marriages? Or did McQuaid's language and approach simply indicate general uneasiness about the greater openness encouraged by the Second Vatican Council and concern as to where such openness might lead? Whatever the reason, it would appear that for McQuaid the youth assembly was a 'no-go' area for Catholics, too dangerous to enter. This ICYA incident does not appear to have been taken up within the ICC. Corry was soon to join the staff of BCC's Youth Department.

Outside Ireland the pace of change was more rapid and far-reaching. For the first time the idea of 'a genuinely universal council', able to reflect the thinking of a wide variety of churches and to speak to the majority of Christians, had been articulated at Uppsala. In addressing the assembly, the Jesuit Roberto Tucci (later to become a Cardinal) referred to the possibility of the RCC joining the WCC, and thought was given to establishing closer relations between the WCC and regional and national Councils of Churches. A symbol of the growing relationship between the WCC and the RCC was Pope Paul VI's visit in 1969 to the recently opened Ecumenical Centre, the building in Geneva that houses the WCC and other inter-church agencies. This was the first such visit by a pope. Further discussion of RC membership in the WCC was, however, quietly shelved in 1972.

Increased co-operation between Catholics and Protestants proved possible in Ireland in a number of uncontroversial areas. Against the background of a sharp rise in violence, we have already discussed the growth in co-operation between those engaged in youth work. There were other examples. First, Christian Preparation for Work Abroad – or more simply, Christians Abroad – was set up as an agency of the BCC and the Conference of British Missionary Societies in May 1969, to prepare Christians accepting secular appointments in Africa, Asia and South America. It ran training courses, supplied sources of information, and commended people to the countries to which they were going. The RC hierarchies in Ireland, Scotland and England approved participation by Catholics. In October 1969, on behalf of the ICC, I took part in a regional Christians Abroad group in Northern Ireland which involved Catholics. Attempts were made to extend the scheme to the South through the ICC/RC Joint Group, on which we report below.

Second, the Uppsala assembly of the WCC had drawn attention to the fact that the rich nations of the world were becoming richer, and the poor nations poorer. In October 1968 the BCC adopted a policy statement on 'Christian Aid and World Development' which sought to point ways forward for individuals, churches and nations. 'In every human being in need', declared the statement, 'we are confronted by Jesus Christ himself.' Providing channels, characterised by integrity and competence, to facilitate responses to world hunger, was presented as a central element in Christian mission springing from the church's nature as the body of Christ. Noel White of the C of I represented the ICC at a conference at Swanwick in October 1969, under the joint sponsorship of the BCC, the Conference of British Missionary Societies and the RCC. Seen essentially as a working consultation, the churches and missionary societies discussed topics such as how to communicate the scale of world poverty; the urgency of the moral challenge; theological arguments for becoming involved; seeing this concern as part of the church's total mission; the responsible use of the churches' financial resources; national objectives; and campaigning methods by and within the churches, locally and nationally. In December 20,000 people in Northern Ireland added their names to a UK-wide Sign-In on World Poverty, in which CA and other agencies co-operated to focus attention on national objectives. There was limited up-take in the South as well. In February 1970 Irish church leaders and administrators discussed the content, aims and follow-up to the Sign-In with Alan Brash (the director of CA), when he visited Cork, Bandon, Killarney, Dublin and Belfast. In the first of two events in Belfast on 4 February Brash met members of the All-Party Parliamentary Committee on World Poverty at Stormont. In the second event he spoke to a gathering of church leaders, executives and trustees from the ICC's member churches, members of the RC Commission on

Justice and Peace and members of CA Committees, and NIV-COAD representatives. The Northern Ireland Voluntary Committee on Overseas Aid and Development was an instrument through which various agencies in Northern Ireland – including Christian Aid, the Freedom from Hunger Campaign, the Irish Students' Development Movement, Oxfam, Save the Children Fund, and War on Want – co-operated on world development issues. The role of Vivian Simpson in both Belfast events was significant. A Methodist local preacher who had worked in Nigeria, he was at this time a N. I. Labour Party MP at Stormont (and was a member of the Tripartite Conversations between the three larger Protestant churches). He was the first chairman of NIVCOAD.

Third, reciprocating a visit by a BCC delegation to East Germany (also known as the DDR or German Democratic Republic) in 1969, a group of twelve representatives from the churches of the DDR came to Britain in November 1970 under the leadership of Bishop Gottfried Noth of Dresden. It was the first ecumenical visit by an East German delegation to Christians in either eastern or western Europe. The ICC acted as hosts to three members of the team – Pastor Dr Theophil Funk (the only Methodist), Pastor Hans Treu (a Lutheran) and Father Walter (the only Roman Catholic) – from 14 to 20 November. With myself accompanying them, meetings took place in Armagh, Coleraine, Londonderry, Belfast and Dublin, with politicians (including leading figures in several political parties), students and religious leaders including the Roman Catholic Archbishops of Armagh and Dublin. Despite his lukewarm ecumenical reputation, the Catholic Archbishop of Dublin graciously received the visitors at his Drumcondra residence. It was a wet and windy day, for which Archbishop McQuaid offered profuse apologies. It was, the East Germans later observed, as if the Archbishop felt that God had let them all down in not granting a more favourable day! They met too with Ian Paisley at Stormont, an encounter in which a junior political colleague of Paisley shared. The latter laughed loudly at Paisley's jokes, but otherwise contributed nothing to the occasion. As the East German visitors later reflected on this encounter, they felt that there were sinister elements in Paisley's overbearing attitude.

He rather reminded them of a domineering politician nearer home who threatened the peace of the world. Altogether the visit was an important exercise in East/West relations, an expression of Christian solidarity and an introduction to the complexities of the Irish situation for church leaders from the DDR.

Fourth, recognising that the ecumenical vision had to be owned more widely by the churches as such, a decision was taken by the ICC to hold an inter-church conference on co-operation to encourage member churches of the Council to re-examine the possibility of increased co-operation on a number of fronts. The proposal was warmly taken up. There were five sections in the conference, social responsibility, education, communication, and mission at home and overseas or world mission. Those from the churches who undertook to chair sections or write reports, agreed to prepare preparatory study material and to be involved in taking the conference's proposals forward. More than eighty people took part in the conference at the Four Courts Hotel, Dublin, during the Week of Prayer for Christian Unity in 1971. They were largely representative of the departmental life of the churches, with observers from local Councils of Churches. Significantly, Roman Catholic consultants and observers also took part, including Canon Robert Murphy, the RC Co-Chairman of the Joint Group, Michael Hurley, and Jerome Connolly of the Commission on Justice and Peace. The conference report, with proposals, was sent to member churches, the Tripartite Conversations, the Joint Group and other appropriate bodies. Follow-up took various forms. Church press officers met to discuss co-operation. In view of the suspension of the publication of the (Methodist) *Irish Christian Advocate* – following bomb damage to its printers – consideration was given to the possibility of a joint C of I/Methodist publication. A working party was appointed to consider the churches' relations with the British Broadcasting Corporation (N. I.). Proposals relating to lay training were passed to relevant church departments. F. N. Warren convened a group to monitor and encourage wider involvement in Ireland in the Week of Prayer for Christian Unity (WPCU), with Brendan Murphy of the RCC and a representative of the Women's World Day of Prayer Committee (WWDP) joining the discussions. A questionnaire was circulated to the churches and account was taken of similar conversations taking place in the BCC and WCC. Suggestions included an Irish inset in annual prayer leaflets; my successor, who was to be appointed on a full-time basis, to be asked to encourage the holding of special inter-church services; the ICC to liaise with the London-based office of WWDP and with area secretaries in Ireland; and the Secretary of the Fellowship of Prayer to be notified of area events for WPCU and WWDP, to encourage greater involvement by both Protestants and Catholics. The possibility of forming an Irish equivalent to the Conference of British Missionary Societies was considered. This later led to the formation of a new world mission committee, with a sharing of information on both Protestant and RC missions.

Within the ICC itself, ecumenical education was seen to be important at all levels to counter fears, misunderstandings and distortions, and to promote and share biblical and ecumenical thinking on inter-church co-operation and cross-community action. Media attention for the ICC was always welcomed. Summary documents were prepared from time to time, to draw attention to Council statements and initiatives, particularly in relation to the Troubles and to peacemaking in the community. A variety of people found these useful, including Council and church members, visitors to Ireland, politicians and others. At its spring meeting in May 1969 the ICC had decided to issue a series of ecumenical pamphlets. The pamphlets were released in the autumn 1969 and soon had to be re-printed. Though written by 'non-Catholics' involved in the work of the Council, Protestant/ Roman Catholic relations were not far from mind in any of the pamphlets and were the particular focus of the third pamphlet:

1 *Christian Unity – What is it?* Professor John Barkley

2 *Christian Unity – Why bother?* Norman Taggart

3 *Christian Unity – What about the Roman Catholic Church?* Carlisle Patterson

4 *Christian Unity – What can we do together locally?* Noel Mackey

5 *What is the Irish Council of Churches?* Robin Richey

6 *What about the World Council of Churches?* Robert Brown

7 *A United Church – Is it Biblical?* Principal James Haire,

8 *Church Union – What is happening in Ireland?* Dr Eric Gallagher.

Inexpensively produced, the pamphlets surveyed the ecumenical scene from an Irish point of view. The journalist John Horgan reviewed them in the *Irish Times*, describing them as a 'useful, attractive and well-written series'. They were widely used, for example as study material for a conference on Christian unity in Dublin in April 1970, organised by the Standing Committee of Women's Church Organisations. PACE quoted extensively from them in successive issues of its bulletin.

CONSULTATION AND CO-OPERATION
IN MORE CONTROVERSIAL AND SENSITIVE AREAS

What of co-operation between Catholics and Protestants in more sensitive and controversial areas such as faith, witness and pastoral care? Much of the remainder of this chapter will be in response to this question. In his pamphlet *Christian Unity – What about the Roman Catholic Church?*, Carlisle Patterson explored in a straightforward and open way the differences and agreements between Catholics and Protestants, and encouraged honest and positive relationships. Surveying the world scene, he indicated ways in which the Catholic Church and other churches – without compromise of doctrine or principle – were working together at different levels on a range of topics such as social change, the marginalised and other local and international issues. Opportunities were being taken, he claimed, to discuss 'with frankness and courtesy' issues at the heart of continuing differences. The relevance to Ireland was clear:

> No one need imagine that there will be swift progress to agreement. There are deeply-held convictions (not merely verbal quibbles or emotional prejudices) on both sides. What we are seeing now is a new openness in encounter, a humble acceptance that no church has in practice lived up to its own doctrines and principles, and a readiness to listen as well as to affirm. These things are characteristic of genuine dialogue. Regrettably, those who assert most loudly the truth of their own position are often most reluctant to talk with those who disagree with them. They fear that 'dialogue' means 'betrayal'. This can happen, however, only if the participants are either ill-informed or uncertain. To shrink from the present opportunites for dialogue is to exhibit, not faithfulness, but

fear ... There are many matters which Irish Christians need to consider together, for the sake of the church and of our whole society. There are disagreements and causes of tension which we ought ... to discuss together in mutual respect and forbearance. There are paths to understanding and renewal which the churches can only explore fully together, in response to the leading of the Spirit and in obedience to Jesus Christ.

Victor Hayward, himself a Baptist, the WCC Associate General Secretary for relations with National Councils of Churches, visited Ireland in March 1970 and addressed the ICC spring meeting. On relations with Roman Catholics he suggested that it was helpful to look at these in a world context. Different nations and regions approached issues such as RC membership of Councils of Churches and mixed marriages in different ways, he acknowledged, yet they could learn from one another. In the end each Council had to find its own way forward.

An opportunity soon arose to encourage sustained Protestant and Catholic study and dialogue. In 1970 the ICC informally and warmly associated itself with the launch of a postgaduate theological institute, the Irish School of Ecumenics (ISE), created to facilitate the study of doctrinal and other aspects of interchurch relations. The ISE is not under official denominational auspices. It was the brainchild of Michael Hurley, as have been other major ecumenical initiatives in Ireland. Hurley's recent comments in *Healing and Hope*, for example about the initial 'official negativity from the Catholic hierarchy' towards the ISE, are revealing.[6] Several of us from the ICC were among the 350 mainly academic and church guests who gathered for the inauguration of the School in Dublin on 9 November, when Dr Carson Blake, a Presbyterian and the General Secretary of the WCC, gave an address on 'The Progress, Promise and Problems of the Ecumenical Movement'. At the dinner afterwards I sat opposite Sean Macbride – a Nobel Peace Prize winner, international jurist and diplomat, and prominent IRA leader in the 20s and 30s – and found the occasion fascinating. The four original Patrons of the ISE were Bishop John Armstrong of the C of I, Professor Barkley of the PCI, Cecil McGarry SJ, and Robert Nelson of the MCI, all serving in a personal capacity. Significantly, two were among their churches' representatives on the ICC and were soon joined by a third. Professor Barkley and Robert Nelson represented the ICC as observers at an international Jesuit conference in Dublin in August 1971.

The Troubles undoubtedly helped to drive the churches closer together. As already noted, discussions had taken place in 1968 about the need for consultation with the RCC in response to community problems. After the serious turn of events in Derry in early January 1969 a special invitation was sent to the C of I Archbishop, the Methodist President and the Presbyterian Moderator to attend a meeting on 8 January from which urgent contact was made with the Prime Minister and a statement was released to the press. A decision was also taken to approach Cardinal Conway, whom Dr Gallagher had already met on 3 January following ICC discussions late the previous year. A confidential letter was sent to the Cardinal from the meeting on 8 January, not in the name of the ICC but signed by seven people on behalf of their churches (all member churches of the Council). It was felt that this was the most appropriate and effective way of proceeding in the circumstances, on account of the suspicion in which ecumenism was held. Apparently, we did our work well. Even thirty years, later Michael Hurley was of the opinion that the letter to the Cardinal looked more like an initiative taken by the church leaders than an ICC initiative.[7] The meeting on 8 January would not, however, have taken place, nor would the letter have been written, had it not been for the Council's initiative, with Dr Gallagher acting on the Council's behalf. The signatories were James McCann, the Church of Ireland Primate; Dr Withers, the Presbyterian Moderator; Gerald Myles, the Methodist President; Albert McElroy, the Non-Subscribing Presbyterian Moderator; Joseph Cooper of the Moravian Church; Lt Col George Snell of the Salvation Army; and Norah Douglas of the Religious Society of Friends (who later settled in Australia following her retirement). Included were these points:

> We write as persons holding positions of major responsibility in our churches and we greet you in the name of our Lord Jesus Christ ... We have long been concerned for the establishment of justice and mutual respect in Northern Ireland (but) recent events have underlined the need for urgent ac-

> tion ... We believe that the achievement of (justice and re-
> spect) may be advanced by a better understanding of each
> other's position and concerns and, where possible, joint ac-
> tion ... There may be advantage from some type of joint con-
> sultative body ... We believe that in normal circumstances
> such a suggestion has much to commend it, but at this pre-
> sent time we are particularly anxious for bridges to be built
> and to be kept open.[8]

Despite a sense of urgency, the signatories added that they realised the Cardinal might like to consult with colleagues before re-
plying. A wish to show respect and not to give offence, coupled
with a concern for the well-being of the Province as a whole at a
time of crisis, was evident. The reference to a 'consultative body'
echoed earlier conversations within ICC circles. The Cardinal
was in England when the letter was sent, but he replied positively
within days to say that he would be pleased to discuss the possibility of joint consultation. He had been 'deeply moved' by the
letter and the statement. They had, he wrote, given him 'great
heart', adding, 'I must express my appreciation of the genuine
spirit of Christianity shown by the Protestant Churches in these
difficult days.'[9] This was a most encouraging response from one
who in the years before the Second Vatican Council, like most on
both sides at the time, had appeared less than enthusiastic about
ecumenical encounter. It reflected increasing confidence and respect among people of different traditions, who were learning to
trust one another and to form closer relations.

A few days later the Roman Catholic hierarchy released its
National Directory on Ecumenism, a short document of twenty-
four paragraphs. It summarised and highlighted aspects of the
Vatican's Directory of two years earlier. Not surprisingly, it contained no reference to the rapidly deteriorating situation within
Northen Ireland. It was on the whole regarded as a rather disap-
pointing document,[10] which however struck this positive note:

> There is in Ireland a new endeavour among Christians of dif-
> ferent denominations to live in harmony and peace. It is to be
> devoutly hoped that this movement will grow and become
> even more permanently permeated by the truth and love of
> Christ.

As a follow-up to the correspondence with the Cardinal, Dr

Gallagher, the ICC Chairman, joined the Church of Ireland Primate and the Presbyterian Moderator in meeting Cardinal Conway on 31 January. The ICC and its Executive Committee were informed of the meeting and developments from it, most notably the setting up of a confidential 'semi-official *ad hoc* Committee'. Thereafter this Committee was known by various names including the 'Heads of Churches Consultative Committee', the 'Church Leaders Consultative Committee' and most fully the '*ad hoc* Church Leaders Consultative Committee on Community Relations.' Each modification reflected variations in emphasis and understanding at different times. The Committee was composed of six clerics, two nominated by the Cardinal, Patrick Walsh (Catholic priest and Chaplain at Queen's University, later to become a bishop) and Denis Faul (Catholic priest and teacher); Harold Allen (Presbyterian minister), nominated by the Government Committee of the PCI; Dr Gallagher, nominated by the President of the MCI; Canon Elliott, nominated by the C of I Primate; and finally John Radcliffe (minister of the Non-Subscribing Presbyterian Church), nominated by the Executive of the ICC on behalf of the smaller churches. The Committee was given the task of keeping in touch with the developing community situation in the North and advising 'their Principals', the church leaders, on joint statements and other initiatives which might be taken. One of its participants, Dr Gallagher, later wrote that the Committee had 'a short, eventful, and occasionally tempestuous history'.[11] The first part of this statement is, however, misleading, given that it is now known that the first meeting of the Committee took place in April 1969 and that the Committee functioned until January 1973. Its existence, wrote Gallagher, was kept confidential because of likely hostility from some quarters. When informed in a private meeting of the Committee's existence, the Home Secretary James Callaghan expressed astonishment that it had been decided to keep this constructive initiative confidential because of likely unfavourable reactions. Around the same time, at a meeting of the ICC Executive Committee in September 1969, I commented that the ICC and its member churches were 'suffering' from 'the policy of non-publicity' understood to have been requested by the Roman Catholic Archbishop. Dr Gallagher expressed the hope that it might soon be possible to change the policy. No change however took place until 1972. The *ad hoc* Committee reported direct to the church leaders (or presumably to the Moderator and / or the Government Committee in the case of the PCI) and to the ICC Executive. The latter took care not to comment on the existence or activity of the Committee in the wider work of the Council, in view of the manner and conditions under which it had been set up. If in reporting to the ICC Executive the *ad hoc* Committee had been able to include an element of consultation, the Executive might have felt less excluded. It would also have helped if in some circumstances there had been more openness about the Committee's existence and work. The Committee had a difficult task, its early meetings being described by one participant as 'the deaf talking to the deaf', but it undoubtedly performed a useful role and bore fruit as fears and grievances were shared. Arguably, the longer it continued the less relevant and helpful it became. Its membership suffered from being totally clerical and Northern-based and as will become evident in these pages, issues were raised by its very existence and ways of operating which proved difficult to resolve.[12]

New attitudes and relationships were possible at a personal level and on less formal occasions. I was invited by the BBC to lead a radio broadcast service on 15 June 1969, to mark the bicentenary of John Wesley's first Methodist Conference in Ireland. Four other Methodists joined me, one lay person, three ministers and all male! More significantly however – given the community situation – was the fact that Michael Hurley also took part through a recorded contribution from Dublin. His words were challenging:

> What the Church and world need are Roman Catholics and Methodists ... who are convinced that to save the world, society or individuals or both, they must be like Jesus in his death; ready to die in order to rise and walk in newness of life, who are sympathetic to each other's difficulties in (the) task of institutional reform and more ready to encourage than to criticise. What the Church and the world of the 60s and 70s need are churches and Christians, Roman Catholics, Methodists and others ... who will 'provoke one another to love and to good works', and who will 'endeavour to help

each other on in whatever we are agreed leads to the king-dom.'[13]

Hurley's quotations at this point in his address came from John Wesley's *A Letter to a Roman Catholic*, originally published in Dublin on 18 July 1749. An edition of the *Letter* had appeared in 1968, edited and introduced by Hurley under the joint imprint of Roman Catholic and Methodist publishers (both private companies), with prefaces by the President of the World Methodist Council and the President of the Vatican Secretariat for Christian Unity. This publication was in itself a considerable ecumenical achievement since we now know that the project was 'nearly still-born', with difficulties arising from 'both sides'.[14] Wesley's emphasis on dialogue and love – 'perfect', practical and unaffected by disagreements – remains vitally important, being central to relations among fellow believers and key to witness and outreach by Christians.

In a broadcast service from Portrush in 1969, Hugh Murphy, a Catholic priest, reflected much of the spirit of Wesley's *Letter* and the Decree on Ecumenism of the second Vatican Council. None was blameless with regard to the Troubles, he acknowledged:

It's so much easier to blame him (my neighbour) rather than myself. He must change. He must make the gesture. He must come round to my way of thinking … What we all need is a change of outlook, for everyone … It's myself I must examine, not the other fellow. It's I who must repent. I must have a change of heart. If we say that we have no sin in us, we are deceiving ourselves and refusing to admit the truth. And to say that we have never sinned is to call God a liar.[15]

As already noted, on 1 May 1969 the ICC instructed its Executive Committee to consider the role of the churches in Irish society. On 28 May its Executive recommended that the Council set up a working party 'to consider … tensions and misunderstanding … and their underlying causes and to (show) how the churches at every level may meet their biblical obligation to promote justice for all sections of the community and to fulfil a reconciling ministry.' Conversations were held with Dr Jack Sayers, editor of the *Belfast Telegraph*, in this connection, to seek his advice and to ask if he himself would be willing to become directly involved. His sudden death brought a sad end to that possibility. Difficulty in obtaining the advice of trained sociologists also caused delay. In a wide-ranging discussion on the future of the Council, at its meeting in Belfast on 6 November, it was emphasised that the Council could not avoid the issue of 'what form of relationship, if any' it should seek with the RCC. The tragic deterioration in events in Northern Ireland and the growth in Catholic/Protestant friendships, required that the issue of official inter-church links with the RCC be faced, not fudged.

In a private session at the same meeting of the Council, the Executive sought and received permission to explore the possibility of joint working parties being set up with the RCC 'on specific problems such as housing, world poverty, causes of tension in the community, employment, the effects of technological and industrial development on human life and environment, Faith and Order etc.' However, in the minutes of the Executive Committee of 8 April the agreed resolution shortened this remit simply to 'advise on the role of the churches in Irish society', though there was also a reference in an accompanying paper to 'social and human problems'. Not surprisingly, therefore, when the proposal to set up a Joint Group was announced in May, its terms of reference fell considerably short of those proposed earlier. The change probably reflected reservations expressed in discussions among Northern Catholic bishops and perhaps within ICC circles. The full statement simultaneously released on 8 May 1970 by Achbishop Simms on behalf of the ICC, and by Cardinal Conway on behalf of the Irish Hierarchy, ran:

> The Executive Committee of the Irish Council of Churches, with the approval of the Council, has agreed to a proposal to set up a Joint Group to be appointed by the member Churches of the Council and the Irish Hierarchy to advise on the role of the Churches in Irish society on such matters as world poverty, employment and housing conditions, drug addiction, alcoholism etc. It is envisaged that separate Working Parties will be set up on individual topics.

Professor John Barkley of the Presbyterian Church later described this initiative as 'most significant'.[16] The inclusion of the 'etc' in the joint announcement gave some hope of flexibility in interpreting the Group's terms of reference. Perhaps in the right circumstances, and as people grew in confidence and became more accustomed to this level and form of co-operation, it might prove possible to tackle other issues such as doctrine and causes of conflict within the community.

The ICC had still to obtain approval for the initiative from the annual meetings of its member churches, after which the churches would be required to appoint their representatives to the Joint Group. In view of Ireland's poor record in Protestant/ Catholic relationships, and the serious political and community situation in Northern Ireland, it would not have been surprising had some problem arisen to prevent progress even at this advanced stage. The ground, however, had been well prepared, and there was in fact little or no opposition when the time came for decision. All member churches gave their approval and eventually made their appointments, the last by 1971. By September 1970 the first meeting of the new body had taken place. There were in all 30 members on the Joint Group, four Church of Ireland representatives; four Presbyterians; two Methodists; one each from the Moravians, Non-Subscribing Presbyterians, Religious Society of Friends and Salvation Army; fifteen Roman Catholics; and myself appointed by the ICC. There were therefore fourteen members from the ICC member churches, with one appointed directly by the ICC making 15 in all, and 15 appointed by the RCC. A large majority of the 30 was based in Northern Ireland. Eleven were lay people, including three women. The officers were Catholic and Protestant in equal numbers, the two Co-Chairmen being Canon Robert Murphy and Dr Gallagher, and the Joint Secretaries Gerard McConville and myself. At the third meeting of the Group on 4 January 1971 good wishes were extended to Robert Murphy on his becoming the first Catholic chaplain to the N. I. parliament at Stormont. This appointment was widely interpreted as a sign both of growing confidence and the benefits of co-operation. An explosion took place at Canon Murphy's home in the autumn 1972, in which he was not injured. It was an abrupt and dangerous reminder of the complex nature of the Troubles.

The Joint Group quickly defined its ways of proceding. Working parties composed of people drawn from different parts of Ireland were to be appointed to undertake specialist work in agreed areas of concern, and would present reports to the Group and (in the case of the ICC) through the Council to its member churches. The need to take into account work already done by the churches and by others, in particular fields, was recognised. The first working party was on drug abuse. It was asked to establish the nature and extent of the problem in Ireland, to collate information, and to make recommendations to the Group, the Council, the churches and other relevant bodies. Its report was presented in 1972. Concern about drugs also prompted the Council to invite Inspector J Scully, Head of the RUC's drug squad, to address its autumn meeting in 1970. Other working parties were appointed as follows, with a note of the year in which reports were presented: housing in Northern Ireland (1973); teenage drinking (1974); under-development in rural Ireland (1976); and most notably in terms of content and media attention, violence in Ireland (1976). Because of differing views and interpretations over the Joint Group's terms of reference, special permission had to be given to enable it to engage in the study of violence.

Work done earlier provided useful resource material for working parties, indicating concerns still needing to be explored. Housing is a good example. A group had already reported on this within the Methodist Church. Housing also exemplified how unforeseen circumstances could upset the smooth running of working parties. Discussions within the ICC led to a working party on housing being set up in February 1970. Later chaired by Tom Boyd, a former NILP MP at Stormont, it was brought under the umbrella of the Joint Group. An interim report was presented in April 1971, when the hope was expressed that a number of old houses could be rehabilitated off the Grosvenor Road, a part of Belfast in which at that time there was a mixed Protestant/Roman Catholic population. The Ministry of Development at Stormont was supportive, and Dr Philbin, the RC Bishop of Down and Connor, indicated he was willing to become involved. The hope was that a successful scheme could be launched through the formation of a shared Churches' Housing Association, with part-funding by the ICC member churches and the RCC. Under the headline 'Bricks and Mortar', the *Belfast Telegraph* warmly welcomed the move as 'a significant break-through' in the social sphere, a sign that the churches were genuinely concerned 'about the human condition' in divided Belfast.[17] Progress was reported to the ICC Executive on 6 May. Houses in Burnaby street were on offer at £100 each, tenants had already been approached, and work was proceeding on drawing up the constitution of a Housing Association. The budget for the purchase and rehabilitation of ten houses looked likely to be in the region of £6,000. Approval was given to form the Housing Association on 23 June 1971. However, at the Executive Committee meeting on 10 September, a major set-back was reported when Dr Gallagher declared that with the introduction of internment and the subsequent upsurge in sectarian violence there was 'now no prospect of the Grosvenor Road area including any kind of integrated housing'. Steps, legal and other, continued to be taken in faith to establish a Churches' Housing Association.

The terms of reference under which the Joint Group operated, and the separate existence and secrecy surrounding the *ad hoc* Committee, continued to be major talking points and indicated a growing sense of unease. Some felt, for example, that the *ad hoc* Committee ought to be made public and be brought under the umbrella of the more open and representative Joint Group. The fact that the two existed side by side created uncertainty and difficulty. At the ICC Executive in April 1971 I expressed concern about the Council's apparent inability 'to initiate any further discussion or action with the Roman Catholic Church in connection with community problems' in Northern Ireland. In the end this could damage the credibility of both bodies, I suggested. At the same time, on behalf of the smaller member churches of the ICC, I expressed regret that they had not been represented in a recent meeting with James Callaghan. It was agreed that these problems should be raised informally with the Cardinal. In May 1971, after attending the *ad hoc* Committee's thirtieth meeting, Dr Weir commented that it had been 'friendly but futile'. Regular members of the Committee might well have viewed things more positively.

I took part in a consultation in Geneva from 28 June to 7 July 1971, involving the WCC and national and regional Councils of Churches, after which I wrote five articles which were fed into

the work of the Council. One, entitled 'Roman Catholic involvement in Councils of Churches',[18] indicated that at a world level
there now appeared to be nothing in RC ecclesiology *per se* to
preclude Catholic membership of Councils of Churches.
Although uncertainties and hesitations remained in some quarters, they appeared to be more of a pastoral or prudential than
theological nature. At local and other sub-national levels in
other parts of the world, I reported, RC membership was increasing rapidly. In Britain, for example, RCs took part in 73 per
cent of more than 700 local Councils of Churches. The RCC was
also a member of ten national Councils of Churches worldwide,
and all the signs were that this trend would continue. Observer
or observer-participant status also existed in other National
Councils, and groups of various kinds enabled Catholics to join
with people from other churches in facing common concerns.
From a Catholic point of view, I continued, such co-operation
appeared to harmonise with the Vatican Council's emphasis on
greater sharing. Joint Groups between RCs and others now
existed in several countries. They often initiated studies on theological issues and topics such as baptism and inter-church marriage as well as social matters. Decisions on forms of co-operation
were being taken by regional Episcopal Conferences in consultation with the Vatican, rather than by the Vatican itself. Turning
to the situation in Ireland, I asked:

> What is the way ahead for us …? Should we not have at least
> an Ad Hoc Group representative of the whole country and of
> all churches willing to co-operate, to advise on the role of the
> Churches on matters related directly to causes of tension
> within the community? The present joint group … valuable
> as it is, appears to have only oblique reference to community
> relations. Possibly its terms of reference and its membership
> could be enlarged to take in this concern … Also, should its
> terms of reference not be widened to enable it to discuss mat-
> ters of faith and practice around which bitter controversy fre-
> quently centres in Ireland …? So long as serious differences
> cannot be responsibly examined, will our co-operation on
> social problems ever be more than superficial?

In referring to the Joint Group and suggesting that a related and
representative group be set up to work openly on other areas of

concern (when there was already an unpublicised body, the *ad hoc* Committee, at work in some of the proposed areas), I was arguably taking a potentially divisive initiative. I saw it as a calculated risk in difficult circumstances, a way of sending out signals to those already 'in the know' about possible new ways of doing things. It was an attempt to encourage fresh thinking and to open up new possibilities, without jeopardising existing programmes.

In view of the widespread fear and misunderstanding concerning Protestant/RC co-operation in Ireland and the initiatives which had been taken in other parts of the world, my statement went on to ask if it was not now time 'to initiate a serious theological examination of the presuppositions and implications of such co-operation' in Ireland? Widening the sphere of discussions and activity posed no threat to the churches, I suggested, since the Joint Group was not itself a decision-making body. Its recommendations had to be referred to the churches and the ICC for discussion, approval or otherwise, and possible action. Repeated reconsideration of the Joint Group's terms of reference and its links with the *ad hoc* Committee, clearly indicate that the assumption that the Irish Group was reluctant or unwilling to confront political and social problems, as has been suggested at times, was unfounded. As is often the case, the reality was much more complex.

In a report to the ICC on 4 November, widely covered in the press,[19] I acknowledged the progress within Ireland in Protest - ant/Catholic contacts of every kind, whether official, semi-official or unofficial. I felt however that much remained to be done:

> As Churches and as a Council, our contacts with the Roman Catholic Church are too few and too slight ... We are only fooling ourselves if we assume that they are anything like adequate. The tragic fact is that the vast majority of Roman Catholics and Protestants in Ireland have little regard for, or understanding of, one another's point of view. The really significant cultural, religious and political influences which determine attitudes remain separatist and sectarian, and render effective co-operation, consultation and mutual criticism difficult if not impossible.

The churches, Catholic and Protestant, and the Council ought to throw their weight behind an urgent attempt to promote respect for one another's views, and to encourage practical co-operation and the honest facing of differences at every level. 'The time for dithering and hedging on this all important (area) had long since passed', I insisted.

The Council considered and accepted the first report of the ICC/RCC Joint Group issued in March 1972.[20] The Group had met on six occasions since September 1970, once in Dundalk, twice in Belfast and three times in Dublin. In each of the first three working parties there were about twenty members, drawn from both jurisdictions, only three or four of whom were members of the Joint Group. Essential liaison between the Group and the working parties was maintained. Liaison with denominational boards and committees was also achieved, where necessary, by asking each one to nominate a representative to each working party. The first report commented on drug abuse, the use of alcohol by young people, housing, service overseas, and the problem of under-development west of the Shannon and the Bann. It also referred directly to discussions on the Group's terms of reference:

> Some, whilst in no way questioning the importance of the subjects that have actually been taken up, feel strongly that a Group appointed to advise the Churches on their role in Irish society, and to enable them to play a developing role in promoting the well-being of society, must concern itself with matters much more directly related to the continuing political and community crisis in Ireland. Others feel tied, however regrettably, to the subjects specifically mentioned in the original announcement ... Some members of the Group are strongly of the opinion that the way must be cleared for the Group to take up some of the key issues – such as violence – which influence actions and attitudes in Ireland today. Clarification on this important matter is therefore being urgently sought.

The Council agreed that this matter be explored with and through the Cardinal and the ICC Executive. In reporting to the annual General Assembly in 1972, the relevant Board of the PCI had no doubt as to where it stood, commenting that in its view it had 'always been quite clear' that 'issues such as violence ...

would in fact fall within the terms of reference' of the Joint Group.

The Executive was kept informed of the work of the church leaders' *ad hoc* Committee on Community Relations following internment. Dr Gallagher reported on 10 September 1971 that both RC members of the Committee were keen to see the SDLP resume normal political activity. The Committee had invited the party to indicate its conditions for returning to Stormont. Referring to earlier discussions about relations between the *ad hoc* Committee and the Joint Group, I reported that some members of the Group felt that their agenda was being 'trivialised' due to the absence from it of 'basic community relations'. Dr Gallagher thought that for the present no further representations could be made to Cardinal Conway on this matter. Clearly different people were coming under different pressures.

At the ICC Executive meeting on 11 October 1971 it was noted that the *ad hoc* Committee was considering 'allegations of torture' surrounding the questioning of internees. On 3 November it was reported that the previous meeting of the *ad hoc* Committee had been 'very unhappy', with Denis Faul speaking at length about alleged cases of torture. Harold Allen had contacted Brian Faulkner on the matter, apparently arguing that the truth would have to be uncovered. 'No cases of undeniable brutality' had as yet come to light, it was reported, 'only a degree of persistence in interrogation' about which there were differences of opinion as to 'propriety'. The tenor of these comments and their similarity to those published weeks later in the Compton Report, as previously noted, were very close. Was this coincidental, or had Allen been given an early indication, officially or otherwise, of what the report was to say? Allen was known to have strong Unionist connections. A lively debate on alleged torture took place within the ICC Executive, in which the Methodist Charles Eyre referred to 'the revulsion' which many church members felt 'at the propaganda onslaught against the military authorities'. It was widely believed within the community that to get at the truth, 'harsh methods' had to be used when questioning suspects. Eyre successfully applied around this time to become a part-time member of the Police Reserve.

At the Executive Committee meeting on 19 November 1971 it

was reported by John Radcliffe and Dr Weir that the *ad hoc* Committee 'had reached an impasse' and had 'got away from fundamental principles and problems'. It was proposed by me and agreed that the members of the *ad hoc* Committee should be asked to suggest to the church leaders that the Committee be dissolved so that the same concerns could be taken up 'by a larger, publicly acknowledged body on an all-Ireland basis.' On 14 January 1972 I reported that the response to this initiative had been 'unclear and fragmentary'. I therefore proposed that 'action be taken to precipitate a definite response'. Dr Gallagher reported the Cardinal's opinion, that the Joint Group – as distinct from the *ad hoc* Committee – could work more successfully if it did not engage in 'the tension-laden area of community relations'. The Cardinal, he went on, had agreed to some public reference now being made to the existence and activity of the *ad hoc* Committee. Robert Brown felt that Presbyterians already believed that the Joint Group's terms of reference included community relations, but, according to Barry Deane, the C of I saw things differently. Had community relations been understood to be included in the remit of the Joint Group, Deane was sure that the C of I would have chosen different representatives. At this point I reminded Executive Committee members of the Joint Group's method of working. The Group provided general oversight and direction, but specialist work was undertaken by working parties to which members were appointed on the basis of their experience and competence in particular areas. If therefore it was agreed that the Joint Group become directly involved in community affairs, it would be through a working party with specialists, clerical and lay, specially brought together for this task.

It was agreed to appoint a sub-committee to consult with the Cardinal on these issues, and to bring proposals to the Executive. Those appointed were Brown, Deane, Nelson and myself. The sub-committee reported on 11 February 1972 and recommended a compromise, first that the *ad hoc* Committee continue but that it be enlarged 'to represent all Ireland and to include lay people'; second that the Joint Group be allowed to study specific aspects of community relations, as approved by the ICC Executive and Cardinal Conway; and third that action was 'urgently needed to search for a structure of consultation and co-operation' with the RCC, to consider 'the long term needs of the Irish situation.' I drew attention to ecumenical bodies within the RCC in Ireland, including the Episcopal Commission on Ecumenism, and suggested that it may in part be the fault of the ICC that contacts had not already been made directly with these. Should the ICC be in touch, for example, with the RC Archbishop of Dublin and the Papal Nuncio? Dr Weir suggested that such changes might prove unsettling to the Joint Group, to which I replied that some in the Joint Group were already frustrated by restrictions to its present agenda. I also reported that Robert Brown, who was absent from the meeting, believed that the Joint Group was the appropriate structure for RC/Protestant consultation, and that any proposed changes should come from it. The Executive agreed to await a response from the Joint Group.

On 13 April it was reported that Archbishop Simms and Principal Haire – the Council's Chairman and his predecessor – had discussed the *ad hoc* Committee's future with the Cardinal. Dr Gallagher was hopeful that things could 'be developed satisfactorily'. By 23 May it was known that the members of the *ad hoc* Committee had decided to ask their Principals 'to revise its terms of reference if it is to continue in existence'. It was now widely recognised that much had changed since the Committee had first been set up in 1969, with the church leaders themselves meeting more frequently and the social and political situation being much more fluid. Neither Dr Gallagher nor John Radcliffe attended the ICC Executive on 30 June 1972, my last meeting. No report was received from the *ad hoc* Committee.

A separate Protestant/Catholic development took place after a visit to Ireland by G. H. Dunne SJ, the General Secretary of SODEPAX (the joint committee on Society, Development and Peace of the RCC and the WCC), with his Associate Secretary Dr Roy Niehall, following the introduction of internment. This led to contacts of a tentative and exploratory nature in the autumn 1971, to see if SODEPAX, in co-operation with the Irish churches and the ICC, could undertake work on a limited scale in the area of community relations. Exploratory interviews of Protestant and RC clergy were carried out by Drs Ron Wiener and John

Bayley of the N. I. Research Institute, employed by SODEPAX on a part-time basis. Some of those interviewed later participated in overnight residential conferences. The officers of SODEPAX wrote to the leaders of the main churches and the ICC, offering to fund a programme for one year under the direction of the N. I. Research Institute, with advisers appointed by the churches, on the understanding that the churches themselves would give 'at least token contributions' towards the costs. The aim was to promote contact between Protestant and Catholic clergy in the interests of community understanding and reconciliation, leaving open the possibility of the laity also becoming involved. Dr Vital Rajan was appointed to work full-time on the project for a year from May 1972. According to Maurice Hayes, Wiener and Bayley – the initial researchers – later 'went native in quite different directions'. Wiener wrote a study on urban development, *The Rape and Plunder of the Shankill,* and Bayley identified closely with republican groups and was later accused of being a British spy.[21]

The topic of inter-church marriages was a contentious and recurring issue. It was, for example, referred to in discussions about the terms of reference of the ICC/RCC Joint Group and in conversation concerning causes of division in society. At the ICC Executive on 3 November 1971, Bishop Armstrong presented a request from the Church Unity Committee of the C of I that the ICC explore the possibility of setting up a body with the RCC to consider joint pastoral care in 'mixed marriages'. This would bring Ireland into line with developments in Britain where the BCC and the RCC in England, Wales and Scotland had created such a body. The MCI made a similar request. Barry Deane suggested that even if the Irish hierarchy was unwilling to take this step, the ICC should examine the question. Archbishop George Simms was at the time Anglican co-Chairman of the Anglican-Roman Catholic International Commission on the Theology of Marriage and its Application to Mixed Marriages, set up in 1968 (which reported in 1975). Dr Weir cautioned the ICC against imagining itself omnicompetent and taking on too much. He also suggested that the appropriate department within the churches to examine the issue would be that concerned with marriage and family issues, not ecumenism. It was agreed to approach member churches and to await their responses. I reported on 11 February that I had received encouraging replies from the churches, and that I would now approach Cardinal Conway. On 16 February I wrote to the Cardinal to request an opportunity to discuss 'the possibility of setting up in Ireland a working party to consider pastoral and other factors involved in inter-Church marriages', as already existed in Britain and elsewhere. I had, I pointed out, received widespread support from ICC member churches for the approach, and had also been asked to discuss whether the ICC could relate to various ecumenical structures within the RCC. For example, was more than 'corresponding contact' possible between the Council and the Episcopal Commission on Ecumenism and its Advisory Committee? On 20 March I reported on my meeting with the Cardinal, in which the main topics had been the terms of reference of the Joint Group and the possibility of three further matters being taken up by the Joint Group, namely the SODEPAX initiative, the study of violence and pastoral problems arising from inter-church marriage. Understandably the Cardinal had indicated that he would have to consult with his colleagues. Meanwhile a further letter had been received by the ICC from the C of I, pressing for action on inter-church marriage. Professor Barkley commented that the annual summer conference at Glenstal was to consider marriage. This might help to move things forward. Mixed marriages remained highly contentious for both sides, however, and 'a serious ecumenical crisis' involving Michael Hurley, the ISE and the Catholic hierarchy was to develop in Dublin in 1973 over arrangements for an international consultation on the issue.[22]

At the spring meeting of the Council in Dublin on 13 April, Barry Deane proposed that inter-church marriage and related matters be taken up with the RCC with greater urgency. The Executive, he argued, should be directed to invite the RCC to nominate representatives to a conference in which issues which 'give rise to tensions or misunderstandings unworthy of relations between different churches' could be identified, with a view to entering into 'detailed discussions on methods of resolving' them. Considerable progress had already been made in the previous two years, he acknowledged, but there was still a long way to go. Acceptance of the motion would give a great fillip to people of goodwill throughout the country. It would also confound those who considered the churches irrelevant to the pressing issues of the day. Dean Charles Gray-Stack seconded the proposal. In response I quoted from the letter I had sent the Cardinal and reported on my meeting with him, commenting that relationships with the RCC were 'being pressed with all urgency'. It would, I suggested, be an 'offence against good taste' and effective diplomacy to push any harder at this point. Dr Gallagher proposed an amendment to Deane's motion, directing the Executive to take whatever positive action was possible following responses to earlier approaches. This was seconded by Robert Brown, and carried. In a 'farewell meeting' with the Cardinal in early June, accompanied by Gerard McConville my co-Secretary of the Joint Group, the Cardinal indicated that the hierarchy in its meeting in June would be considering relations with the member churches of the ICC. At my final ICC Executive meeting on 30 June I reported that the signs were that the hierarchy would propose wide-ranging discussions, with nothing ruled out.

I always found Cardinal Conway interested and responsive. On one visit, for example, I found him reading Eberhard Bethge's biography of Dietrich Bonhoeffer (published in 1970). Twenty years earlier, before the Second Vatican Council and long before becoming Cardinal, Conway had written of the dangers of 'round-table' conferences since they might convey the impression that 'in accepting merely equal rights' Catholics could give the impression that 'they accept the principle that the Catholic Church is on an equal footing with other religious bodies.'[23] In this he had reflected the spirit of the times. A naturally cautious man, he proved to be open to persuasion and had returned from the Second Vatican Council fully committed to its vision and determined to implement its decrees in Ireland, despite understandable hesitation from some quarters.

The response from the RC Episcopal Conference duly arrived in July. It came from the Secretary of the Irish Hierarchy, the Bishop of Meath, Dr McCormack. Quite a remarkable document, it re-echoed in some ways Deane's earlier call from within the ICC for an inter-church conference. In effect what the hierarchy proposed was a form of round-table conference in which ecumenism was open for discussion:

> At a meeting of the Irish Episcopal Conference held last month the bishops decided to invite representatives of the Protestant Churches in Ireland to a joint meeting at which the whole field of ecumenism in Ireland might be surveyed.

> What is contemplated is a general review of relations between the Christian Churches in Ireland and the possibilities of further dialogue on both practical and doctrinal issues, including the various matters raised in Reverend Norman Taggart's letter of the 16th February last. It is envisaged that working parties might subsequently be set up to further such dialogue.

> It was suggested that the good offices of the Irish Council of Churches might be availed of to arrange for a corresponding representative group of its member churches to attend such a meeting with the Irish Episcopal Conference. The time and place of the meeting would be a matter for subsequent arrangement.[24]

This response implied that there would be no participation by the ICC as such in the proposed meeting, in effect treating the ICC as a 'post box'. There was, however, time for this to be reconsidered. It was also open to ICC member churches to ensure that some of those who represented them on the Council were included in their teams to take part in the Inter-Church Meeting.

The Catholic hierarchy had hoped for a meeting soon after their next scheduled conference in October 1972. This, however, proved impossible from an ICC point of view since the main decision-making bodies of its member churches – required in some cases to endorse acceptance of the invitation – would not be meeting again until the spring or early summer 1973. This was true for example of the General Assembly of the PCI and the annual Conference of the MCI. After further preparatory work and endorsement by the ICC member churches (with some difficulty in the case of the PCI), the first Irish Inter-Church Meeting (IICM), as it became known, eventually took place on 26 September 1973 between the ICC member churches and the Irish Episcopal Conference of the RCC. The series of meetings was also referred to as 'the Ballymascanlon Talks', being held at the Ballymascanlon hotel near Dundalk.

The meeting in September 1973 was 'epoch making' according to Professor Barkley. An article in the *Irish Catholic Directory 1974* spoke of it as inaugurating 'a whole new era in Catholic-Protestant relations'. An ICC publication described it as 'an enormous step forward in interchurch relations'. Cardinal Conway welcomed it as a 'very significant ... advance'. Bishop (later Archbishop) Cahal Daly and Dr Stanley Worrall (a Methodist Local Preacher and Headmaster of Methodist College) together wrote of it 'as an historic moment in the history of the Christian Churches in Ireland'.[25] Others, however, were more cautious. John Cooney, the journalist and broadcaster, for example, wrote in guarded terms. To him the first meeting marked the start of 'a possible new era in Irish church history', following what could be described as a lost year since the invitation had first been issued. 'Only the most sanguine devotee anticipates that anything dramatic will arise', he added. To him some of the signs were not encouraging, including unawareness of one another's churches; tradition and protocol stifling inspiration; evidence of anti-ecumenism; evidence too of ecumenical uncertainty, suspicion and administrative weakness; and a lack of ecumenical urgency and serious commitment. He was in no doubt as to the challenge facing the churches:

> The standing of the Irish Churches is under question from the dual crisis of the Northern Ireland situation and the growing secularisation of Irish society, both North and South. September 26 is as much a test of the credibility of the Irish churches as it is of their ecumenical seriousness.[26]

Insiders and outsiders will have regarded the first meeting with a mixture of hope, fear and uncertainty. Various influences and movements, the ICC among them, had helped to create a rare moment of opportunity. It was a time when differing churches and traditions could commit themselves to a journey together in faith, discovery and hope; a time too, to demonstrate willingness to face differences and build trust, and to work for societies in both parts of Ireland which could become more open, just, caring and peaceful. Those familiar with the churches and the enormity of the task confronting them, would have known that for deep, lasting and radical results to flow from the initiative, participants were likely to have to be together for 'a long haul', not 'a quick fix'. A new, difficult but potentially productive era had begun.

How did the IICM affect the role of the ICC/RCC Joint Group and the *ad hoc* Committee on Social Problems? The post-1972 situation is discussed by Ian Ellis and Michael Hurley in *The Irish Inter-Church Meeting, Background and Development*, published by the IICM in 1998. There we learn that the Joint Group existed alongside the IICM – the work of the two remaining unco-ordinated – until the mid 80s, when the Joint Group became part of a new Department of Social Issues within the IICM.[27] Ellis and Hurley make no mention of the *ad hoc* Committee after 1972. This is not surprising, given that the discussions and tensions to which it gave rise have till now been so little reported. Bishop Patrick Walsh and Denis Faul, the two Catholic members, are the *ad hoc* Committee's sole surviving members. According to Bishop Walsh, there were in all more than thirty meetings of the Committee, the first on 23 April 1969 and the last on 12 January 1973. As he remembers, no formal closure took place. The meetings simply came to end, without, one suspects, an acknowledgment of the work done by members of the Committee. It is hoped that a full account of the Committee will be written.

CHAPTER 4

The ICC: Successes, Criticisms and Challenges

In assessing the success or otherwise of the Irish Council of Churches, we have to reckon with the fact that 'success' and 'failure' are relative terms as the cross and the 'upside down values' of the kingdon remind us. This is not to say that progress cannot be measured against goals set and hopes raised. What evidence is there of success in the life of the ICC between 1968 and 1972?

Annual reports presented to the General Assembly of the PCI pointed to a gathering pace in the life of the Council. After drawing attention to my imminent appointment as Organising Secretary of the ICC in 1968 and a list of tasks for the Council's part-time staff (Robin Richey and myself), the report urged that 'the development of the work of the (Council) must be one of our top priorities'. In 1969 reference was made to my 'vision and initiative' already 'bearing fruit'. In 1970 it was noted that the work of the Council continued 'to gather momentum'. The following year the annual report spoke of a 'rapid escalation' in the ICC's activities, and outlined and commended proposals 'to make the Council a much more effective instrument of the churches working together'. The Council, the report continued, 'stands on the threshold of what could be a period of most effective service'. In 1972, after drawing attention to the tragic and rapidly deteriorating situation within the community which profoundly affected the churches' witness, the report proceeded to acknowledge the role of the ICC in responding to expressions of concern, offers of help and requests for information from people and churches around the world.

As already indicated, in appointing me as its part-time Secretary the Council emphasised that main areas of ICC activity included ecumenical education, liaison with the BCC and other

Councils of Churches, encouraging co-operation between Irish churches and their departments, monitoring new relationships between Irish churches including the RCC, and improving the efficiency of the Council. Progress was made on each of these fronts though no one would deny that more could and should have been done. Robin Richey took the lead on the administrative side. Despite a considerable increase in the Council's activity, he was able to keep abreast of developments, convening and making arrangements for meetings, and writing and circulating the minutes. Committee minutes are frequently under-rated. His were accurate, noted main concerns, recorded decisions, often gave clues to the 'feel' of meetings and indicated action to be taken. They seldom had to be amended and have greatly facilitated the writing of this work.

Our main focus here has been on the ICC's response to the community and political crisis and on its growing links with the churches, most notably the RCC. The Council did not simply monitor new relations between Irish churches, as urged, but took initiatives in encouraging and promoting them. Relations with the RCC increased greatly, the Council helping to prepare the ground for the unpublicised *ad hoc* Committee to be set up and being a full partner in creating, servicing and giving direction to the Joint ICC/RCC Group with its various working parties. As we have seen, this helped to prepare the way for the first Irish Inter-Church meeting in 1973. There were other developments with Catholics, including the launch of the Irish School of Ecumenics, being represented at an international Jesuit conference in Dublin, supporting joint Catholic/Protestant youth programmes, and helping to put the contentious issue of inter-church marriage on the agenda of Catholic/Protestant discussions. The Four Courts conference located ecumenism more firmly within the departmental life of the member churches, and benefitted from Catholic involvement. In the information seminar on the Irish crisis held at Whiteabbey, intended primarily for media people from the European churches, care was taken to involve people of influence, including Catholics, from the churches and community. Liaison with the BCC, the WCC and other Councils increased. The visit by three East German Christians – Catholic, Lutheran and Methodist – was a 'first' and created a high level of interest. A wide variety of people, North and South, took part in their programme.

I clearly recall – though I cannot now find 'chapter' and 'verse' – that early in my time with the Council there was a reluctance to speak of the need for political change and reform in Northern Ireland, lest this be taken as a sell-out to Nationalists on the constitutional issue. Yet the ICC stuck to its task despite the alarming drift into violence in the community and differences and tensions within and beyond the Council, sustaining a consistent and deepening commitment to the need to respect all legitimately held political opinion. Though conscious that its links with the North were stronger than those with the South, the Council sought to steer clear of taking sides on the national question, believing that this question was a matter which could only be resolved through normal political, legal and peaceful processes. The ICC's policy was to press by word, action and example for the creation of more just, open and caring societies in both parts of Ireland. To help achieve this, it initiated contacts with a wide range of politicians and community leaders, and – believing that unilateral government was no longer acceptable – it called for cross-community approaches to problems. That it was able to provide a 'safe space' for discussions, stretching as they did to robust debate on occasions, on potentially divisive issues like fears and grievances, government and unity by consent, alternative forms of democracy, peace with justice and the demands of pluralism, whilst at the same time taking care to respect member churches' sensitivities, was nothing short of remarkable.

The quality of the ICC's 'top' leadership was crucial in keeping the Council on course, with Dr Gallagher, Principal Haire and Archbishop Simms its successive Chairmen. Different in approach and style, they respected and complemented one another. Being in turn Methodist President, Presbyterian Moderator and Church of Ireland Primate enhanced the Council's standing within the churches and added to its witness within the community. Gallagher was deeply grounded in the Northern situation – he never served in the Republic, which in those days was fairly unusual for Methodist ministers (though he had studied at Trinity College) – and was arguably the leading churchman of his generation. He was President of the MCI from 1967 to 1968. No one showed greater concern than he to interpret and apply the gospel to Ireland's divided society, North and South, nor possessed a stronger instinct for what was necessary and possible in most difficult circumstances. Principal James Haire was Moderator of the PCI from 1970 to 1971, and had to resume office from January to June 1972 following the death of his successor as Moderator. An able and discerning theologian, his wise and genial leadership of the Council was a great source of strength. He was succeeded in the chair by Archbishop George Simms, a scholarly and deeply spiritual person who combined gentleness and strength to an unusual degree. He remained uncomplaining and loyal to ecumenical colleagues despite unfair criticism in the media following the release of an inter-church statement appearing to welcome the introduction of internment. He enjoyed the respect and confidence of his near neighbour, Cardinal Conway, and with his wife, Mercy, was ideally placed to contribute to the Council's growing contacts with the RCC.

At times the work of the Council was valued beyond the churches. Shirley Williams, for example, when a Labour MP and Junior Minister in the Home Office at Westminster, wrote to the General Secretary of the BCC to say that 'throughout the recent disorders Her Majesty's Government have appreciated the assistance of those who, like the Irish Council of Churches, have spoken out in favour of moderation and tolerance.'[1]

CRITICISMS

Inevitably the ICC also had its critics. Criticisms could be prejudiced and ill-informed – on occasions deliberately so, one suspects – presenting a caricature of the truth. Genuine misunderstanding and misperceptions also played a part, when misleading and unhelpful statements – sometimes by ecumenical enthusiasts, among others – confused the issues. Only by patience, clear thinking, open sharing and God's grace (the latter, above all) can such difficulties be resolved.

Misunderstanding surrounds the search for Christian unity and the implications of membership in Councils of Churches whether at local, national, regional or world level. Membership does not imply that a church turns its back on its own doctrinal stance and traditions, or that it accepts the doctrinal position or even the 'full ecclesial status' of other churches. Councils of Churches exist precisely to enable member churches which differ to consult and to gain greater understanding and appreciation of one another's positions, and, whenever possible, to work together on agreed programmes of discovery, witness and service. Member churches, it must be emphasised, are not committed to approve specific actions or statements by Councils. Churches fully retain their own autonomy of judgement and action in such matters. On the other hand, churches which are indifferent or even hostile to the ecumenical movement, or who withdraw from Councils for any reason (conscience, theology or whatever), are in danger of isolationism, self-justification and, most seriously, of acting contrary to New Testament teaching. They deny to themselves the stimulus of regular contact with churches and traditions which, though differing from their own, also claim the name of Christ and may have perspectives and riches to share with them. They forfeit regular opportunities to witness to those with whom they differ concerning their own convictions, values, traditions and insights. The series of Irish ecumenical pamphlets was an attempt to respond to this range of issues and to explore the relation between mission and unity. Disunity among Christians, I wrote in the second pamphlet, distorts truth, wastes resources, hinders witness, impoverishes worship and discredits the gospel, and I continued:

> Fundamental questions remain to be answered. What right have we to proclaim a gospel of reconciliation to a divided community in a divided world when we ourselves within the church are unreconciled? Is it not a denial of the gospel itself to have to say of other Christians, 'we are not in communion with them' and 'of course we don't have much in common with them'? The search for visible forms of unity is not a distraction from the task of proclaiming the gospel. Far from it. It is an essential part of our response to the gospel, and unless we find (ways) of expressing our unity in Christ we shall remain what we must now appear in the eyes of the world – insincere preachers proclaiming a gospel that does not work.

Quite properly, the ICC's sharpest critics were among those who were most centrally involved in its work. Dr Weir frequently called into question the need or wisdom of the Council to engage in new areas of concern. He also regularly reminded the Council and its officers of limits to the ICC's influence with bodies such as the BCC and WCC. The ICC, he insisted, must not usurp the rights of member churches of those bodies in relating directly to other Councils of Churches. This applied to the C of I, the MCI and the PCI, at the time all member churches of the BCC and WCC as well as of the ICC. The ICC's role in relating to other Councils was in his view different, perhaps less important, than that of member churches. At the same time he would have been aware that the WCC – which had started as 'a Council of Churches' – was at the time re-examining all its relationships in the light of the rapid growth in numbers and influence of regional and national Councils of Churches. To an extent what was evident here was a lack of trust, coupled with Weir's need to demonstrate within Presbyterianism that as General Secretary of the PCI he put his own church first at a time when the PCI's ecumenical commitment was coming under strain. Frequent reminders by him of the ICC's limitations and restrictions were, however, a source of irritation to those already well aware of them, and may have caused complications in contacts with Catholics and others not familiar with the kind of sensitivities involved. In March 1972, for example, after referring to complicated structures within the RCC and limits to the ICC's authority in speaking on behalf of its member churches, Dr Gallagher allowed his irritation to show when he commented, 'often I despair of Church co-operation'. As already observed, Weir sometimes expressed criticism about the balance of the Council's work. Was it becoming too politically oriented, he wondered? At the Council Executive in October 1971, for example, he spoke of the danger of the Council's activity 'degenerating into political diplomacy' with the gospel forgotten and 'spiritual, religious and even (church) duties and interests' disappearing from view. People, he said, are beginning to 'feel that the gospel is not applicable to a war situation'. The report of the working party on evangelism, presented five months earlier, had however pointed to a form of piety in the North which lacked 'the living heart of faith' and tended to accept 'uncritically the political *status quo*'. The gospel in every society needs to be interpreted and applied in changing contexts. One suspects that in Ireland, North and South, the member churches of the ICC, particularly the larger ones, were in greater danger than their lowly ecumenical instrument of having an unhealthy interest and entanglement in politics.

To be fair, Dr Weir never allowed personal differences or disagreements to mar relationships. He was a good colleague who represented his church well, often enabling the Council to anticipate likely pitfalls and obstacles when presenting proposals to the churches. He was to display great courage when in late 1974 he took part in secret talks between Protestant churchmen and members of the Provisional IRA Army Council in Feakle, county Clare. We note, in passing, that the event at Feakle did not take place in a vacuum. The majority of those involved on the Protestant side have featured in these pages or were successors of others who have done.

When Dr Gallagher stepped down as Chair of the ICC in November 1969, and again in March 1970 when he presented an interim report on re-structuring the ICC, he noted the progress the Council had made and at the same time discussed critical questions concerning its future. The churches now had a Council they could use, to their benefit and that of the community, yet they seldom commissioned work from it and the Council itself seemed reluctant to make its mind known to the churches:

> The reason may be complicated – part reluctance (by) the Churches to surrender their own freedoms, part reluctance of the Council to act or speak, possibly due to suspicion from the Churches or whatever ... Perish the thought that the Council should simply reflect the thinking of the average Church member in the average Church. On the other hand, I know that we dare not be so radical or irresponsible in our pronouncements as to be completely mistrusted. Here is the tension in which the Council must always live – so to speak as to command the confidence of the Churches and yet to lead their thought and action.[2]

I too made critical comments following my visit to Geneva in July 1971 for a consultation on national and regional Councils of Churches. There was, I reported, a feeling in some quarters that conservatives had taken control of Councils to prevent things happening or to lessen the pace of change, using ecumenical structures as facades behind which church representatives remained as uncommitted ecumenically as in the past. The main responsibility for encouraging church members to think and act ecumenically lay with member churches, not Councils, I suggested. In my final report as Organising Secretary in April 1972, I focused on the connection between the Council and its member churches believing that it could have a crucial bearing on the churches' ability 'to engage creatively in matters of vital national importance'. In Ireland, I suggested, there had been a tendency to regard the ICC as 'a convenient and harmless talk shop' into which ecumenical enthusiasts could safely be diverted while the real work of the kingdom was carried on through denominations for which God himself was somehow thought to be directly responsible. A new approach was now required. Seldom requested by the member churches to do work on their behalf:

> we have … tended to be self generating, doing those things which for one reason or another we felt to be important; and when we have come to our conclusions and written our reports it has not been easy to feed these into the (mainstream) of the Churches even when the Churches themselves, or prominent individuals in them, have acknowledged that what we had done is valuable … We have tended to become an institution separate from the Churches when … we were intended to be an instrument of the Churches.[3]

In commenting on church responses to the crisis within Ireland, it was often only a 'denominational story' which church papers told, I said. 'Should it not be normal practice for all member churches of the Council to claim the work of the Council as their own?', I asked. Acknowledging that some churches might fear the Council becoming too powerful I continued:

> In no sense ought the Council to be feared as a rival either to the Churches themselves or to their departments … (The Council) must not be allowed to seek such power … which would place an intolerable burden on its relationships with its member Churches, and would make it difficult for it to fulfil its essential task of being mediator and critic within and between the Churches and within the community on behalf of the Churches. What the Churches should provide it with is

> an agenda and the means to tackle it, and the assurance that when it has completed its work … in any field the Churches themselves will take serious note of what it has to say … As the Churches work out this new kind of relationship with their own Council, they will have to keep under constant review the work of their own denominational structures. (This) will be seen as a corollary to voluntary participation in the … Council.

With hindsight, I regret that the statement failed to give adequate emphasis to the Council's servant role, and I suspect I rather clouded central issues by making distracting references to the Council's financial and staffing needs.

In an article published in the summer 1972 I emphasised the need for what I called 'informed confrontation' between Protestants and Catholics, sensing that perhaps too little attention had been paid to this earlier:

> There must be greater opportunity for … honest and informed confrontation on the significant points of difference in faith and practice … which still divide. Perhaps it is our failure to speak candidly of such differences, and our desire to be seen to be doing things together rather than always appearing to be bickering about our differences, that has been responsible for giving the mistaken impression that in our ecumenical zeal we do not care for truth. It would certainly be my own contention that in the future, consultation and co-operation can only be on an increasingly superficial level if we rule out the honest examination of fears and differences.[4]

A quarter century later, a short address at an event marking the celebration of the 75th anniversary of the UCCI and the ICC enabled me to re-visit earlier criticisms of the ICC between 1968 and 1972:

> I shared in the vision and uncertainties of those days, believing that what we were attempting was important for the Churches and the wider community. I must also admit to a growing doubt … Were ecumenical instruments, including the ICC, genuine instruments of change? Or were they, in the hands of some church administrators, instruments to control change at a pace acceptable only to conservatives?[5]

What of Ian Paisley? He has featured in these pages, not surpris-

ingly given his strident anti-Catholicism, anti-ecumenism and
resistance to political reform and closer contacts with the
Republic. Should the ICC have done more to challenge his views
and influence? With the benefit of hindsight, perhaps it should. I
can only recall a few occasions when direct reference was made
to him in our conversations. The unspoken assumption was that
Paisley should not be given greater publicity than he was already receiving, recognising that he relished political and religious controversy and was a master of the half truth and at
manipulating people's fears to his own advantage. For tactical
reasons, confrontation was therefore avoided as far as possible,
being regarded as highly damaging to Christian witness.
Helping to heal community division was recognised as a priority
in the Council, to be pursued in indirect and low key ways in
difficult circumstances. When therefore in 1969 Gordon Gray
called upon the Council Executive to examine urgently with
Catholics the holding of 'a large scale public event' to express 'in
a dramatic manner' the concern of the churches for 'community
reconciliation ... based on justice and mutual respect', the majority opinion was that such a high profile initiative could do
more harm than good, for example by inevitably drawing attention to the existence of both liberal and 'Paisleyite' elements
within the mainline Protestant churches. Gray's initiative
prompted a further call by the ICC to church and community
leaders, 'to consider as a matter of great urgency how they could
contribute to ... social reconciliation.' It is known that from time
to time individuals – church people and others – made personal
overtures towards Paisley, in the hope of having unpublicised
conversations with him. More often than not they were ignored
or challenged to take part in high profile public debate. Some of
those who openly voiced criticisms of Paisley received abusive
and threatening messages. The Council's main response to
Paisley was, first, to endeavour to draw attention to the Bible's
teaching on themes such as Christian unity, reconciliation,
peace, justice, forgiveness and community building. Second, the
Council sought to challenge politicians and others to apply solely
peaceful methods to political problems, and to work to create
more inclusive and open societies in both parts of Ireland. Third,
the ICC encouraged churches to work together as far as con-

science would allow in terms of the Lund principle, for the good of society and Christ's kingdom. Dating back to the third Faith and Order conference at Lund, Sweden, in 1952, the principle posed the question whether the churches 'should not act together in all matters except those in which deep differences of conviction compel them to act separately?'

CHALLENGES

What of the future? Many of the issues which have emerged in these pages ought to remain on the churches' agenda. These include the need for an informed, open, loving and honest facing of continuing differences within and between churches; the primary responsibility of churches to enable their members to live ecumenically, valuing and respecting those with whom they differ, whether within the same tradition or another; encouraging local congregations to relate in practical ways to others, including nowadays people of other faiths, as a normal part of Christian living; and examining and responding in a Christian manner to separatist and sectarian institutions and influences, which still mould people's attitudes and actions in both parts of Ireland. In community and political terms, whatever our church and the orgaanisations to which we belong, our chief loyalty is always to Christ and his kingdom. We are to love the Lord our God with our whole being and our neighbour as ourselves (Matthew 22:37-40). Fully engaged in everyday living, we are not to forget that we are citizens of heaven. In every situation and circumstance, we are required to 'act justly ... to love mercy and to walk humbly with (our) God' (Micah 6:8).

Churches today need to face the fact that in the New Testament unity, not disunity, is the gospel ideal. The search for unity as and how Christ wills, ought always to be a Christian priority. In March 1968 representatives from the C of I, the MCI and the PCI, who were engaged in three way talks – the Tripartite Conversations – published a Declaration of Intent, which was endorsed by the three churches and then promptly forgotten. It remains valid and challenging. Five brief comments made by me at the time and based on the declaration, are still in order.[6] First, the declaration implied that the journey towards unity would be long and painful. It required repentance and change, both of them difficult. Second, it left open the form such unity should take, seeking only what was in harmony with God's will. Third, it expressed the conviction that unity is God's will and gift. This truth – needing to be affirmed and declared in every age, whatever the circumstances – lifts unity from the realm of the impossible to the realm of the assured. Fourth, it called the churches to seek the unity which Christ wills, through encounter with one another in prayer, study and action prompted by the Spirit. Fifth, the declaration linked the unity of the church to Christ's mission in the world. Unity is always and only for the glory of God and the sake of the world. Searching questions still confront us. Do we stand by these principles? How do our present ways of relating to one another measure up to the fullness of God's purpose, promises and gifts? Has he not much more to give us? Have we not much more to receive? Is not the crunch issue today, how can we best 'serve the present age'? What is our mission, and how should we set about it? 'He made known to us the mystery of his will … which he purposed in Christ … to bring all things in heaven and on earth under one head, even Christ' (Ephesians 1: 9-10). How long, Lord?

Notes and References

CHAPTER 1: A PERSONAL PERSPECTIVE

1. 'Arminianism' describes the Methodist emphasis on the universality of the offer of salvation and the freedom of individuals to accept or reject it. The Dutch theologian Arminius (1560-1609), whose writings Wesley had read, challenged the Calvinist teaching that salvation is available only to the 'elect', referring to those who are predestined to receive it. The phrase 'the optimism of grace' recurs in Methodist writings. J. M. Turner, for example, distinguishes between the 'optimism of nature', the Enlightenment view that humanity was fundamentally good; the 'pessimism of grace', the Calvinist view that humanity was fundamentally evil with some saved through God's elective grace; and the 'optimism of grace', Wesley's view that no limits could be put to what God can do in human hearts and relations through his grace offered to all (J. M. Turner, *John Wesley, the Evangelical Revival and the Rise of Methodism in England* (2002), p. 76.

2. N. W. Taggart, *The Irish in World Methodism 1760-1900*, 1986, p. X.

3. This is discussed in chapter 2, pp. 80-2.

4. The *Sligo Champion*, 12 July 1968.

5. The *Irish Christian Advocate*, 16 January and 6 February 1969.

6. The minute book of the Carrickfergus Circuit, Quarterly meeting held in Greenisland on 1 June 1972.

CHAPTER 2: THE ICC AND THE NORTHERN IRELAND CRISIS

1. R. English, *Armed Struggle, The History of the IRA*, 2003, p. 98.

2. Taken from a summary of the Council's Statements and Actions 1968-71, pp. 1-2.

3. P. Bew and G. Gillespie, *Northern Ireland: A Chronology of the Troubles 1968-99*, 1999, p. 4.

4. T. O'Neill, *The Autobiogaphy*, 1972, pp. 115-6; and minutes of the Belfast Council of Churches.

5. Bew and Gillespie, op. cit., p. 6.

6. O'Neill, op. cit., pp. 145-9.

7. Taggart, private papers.

8. K Bloomfield, *Stormont in Crisis, A Memoir*, 1994, pp. 100-3.

9. Gallagher, private papers. A copy of Taggart's letter to Ardill is in Taggart, private papers.

10. Taggart, private papers, address by Gallagher.

11. Taggart, private papers, sermon by Taggart.

12. Taggart, private papers, letter to *Theology*.

13. Gallagher, private papers.

14. A. Gailey, *Crying in the Wilderness*, 1995, pp. 158-9.

15. B. Mayne, *Changing Scenes*, 2003, pp. 132-3.

16. D. McKittrick and D. McVea, *Making Sense of the Troubles,* 2001, p. 33.

17. Taggart, private papers, address by Gallagher.

18. R. English, op.cit., p. 133.

19. Ibid., p. 119.

20. Taggart, private papers, letter to C of I, MCI and PCI leaders.

21. Gallagher, private papers.

22. M. Hayes, *Minority Verdict,* 1995, p. 84.

23. Taggart, private papers.

24. Forty-ninth annual report, ICC, p. 11.

25. B. Faulkner, *Memoirs of a Statesman,* 1978, p. 74.

26. I summarised these in a sermon in Greenisland on 'Biblical Protestantism', widely covered in the media. See the *Irish Christian Advocate*, 3 September 1970.

27. Fiftieth annual report, ICC, pp. 8-9. See also forty-eighth report, p. 8, and forty-ninth report, p. 13.

28. Faulkner, op. cit., p. 118.

29. D. McKittrick, S. Kelters, B. Feeney and C. Thornton, *Lost Lives,* 1999, p. 80.

30. Bew and Gillespie, op. cit., p. 39.

31. None of the church leaders attended the meeting which produced the statement. See p. 54.

32. Taggart, private papers.

33. Taggart, private papers, Deane's written speech.

34. Bishop Walsh made this point in conversation with me.

35. Gallagher, private papers.

36. The letters are in Taggart, private papers.

37. Hayes, op.cit., p. 156.

38. Ibid, p. 82.

39. The *East Antrim Times,* 17 September 1971.

40. For coverage of the seminar, see, for example, the *Belfast Telegraph,* 3 and 4 December 1971; the *News Letter,* 2 and 6 December; the *East Antrim Times,* 3 December; and the *Methodist Recorder,* 16 December.

41. Bew and Gillespie, op.cit., p. 45.

42. J. Morrow, *On the Road of Reconciliation*, 2003, p. 39.

43. R. English, op. cit., p. 153.

44. The *Belfast Telegraph*, 7 January 1972.

45. The *Irish News*, 24 January 1972.

46. Taggart, private papers, letter from 'F. White'.

47. See, for example, coverage in the *East Antrim Times*, 11 February 1972; the *Belfast Telegraph*, 12 February; and Taggart, private papers.

48. The *Irish Times*, 14 April 1972.

49. This summary of the April meeting of Council is partly based on reports in the *Irish Press*, 14 April 1972; the *Irish Times*, 14 April; and the *Church of Ireland Gazette*, 21 April.

50. E. Gallagher and S. Worrall, *Christians in Ulster 1968-1980*, 1982, pp. 68-9.

51. The *Irish Times*, 14 April 1972.

52. Taggart, private papers.

53. B. Mayne, op. cit., p. 115.

54. See, for example, coverage in the *News Letter* and the *Belfast Telegraph* on 12 June 1972; and the *Irish Times* on 13 June. I kept notes on telephone calls received (Taggart, private papers).

55. The *Methodist Recorder*, 7, 14, 21 and 28 December 1972.

CHAPTER 3: THE ICC AND THE ROMAN CATHOLIC CHURCH

1. M. Hurley and I. Ellis, *The Irish Inter-Church Meeting*, 1998, pp. 5-6.

2. Ibid., p. 4.

3. M. Hurley, *Healing and Hope, Memories of an Irish Ecumenist*, 2003, p. 74.

4. J. Cooney, *John Charles McQuaid, Ruler of Catholic Ireland*, 1999, p. 371; I. Ellis, *Vision and Reality, A Survey of twentieth century Irish Inter-Church Relations*, 1992, p. 119.

5. J. Cooney, op.cit., p. 408f.

6. Hurley, *Healing and Hope*, p. 87.

7. Hurley and Ellis, op.cit., p. 18.

8. Taggart, private papers.

9. Gallagher, private papers.

10. Hurley and Ellis, op.cit., pp. 17 and 35 (note 74).

11. Gallagher and Worrall, *Christians in Ulster 1968-1980*, 1982, p. 133.

12. I am particularly grateful to Bishop Patrick Walsh for the light he has thrown in conversation on the role and work of the *ad hoc* Committee. Previous treatments of the subject have been unsatisfactory.

We need a fuller, documented account.

13. Taggart, private papers, the BBC script.

14. Hurley, *Healing and Hope*, p. 79.

15. Quoted in my sermon on 'Biblical Protestantism', referred to in note 26 under chapter 2, as reported in the *Irish Christian Advocate*, 3 September 1970.

16. J. M. Barkley, *The Irish Council of Churches 1923-1983*, 1983, p. 26.

17. The *Belfast Telegraph*, 17 April 1971.

18. Taggart, private papers.

19. See for example the *News Letter*, 6 November 1971; and the *Church of Ireland Gazette*, 12 November.

20. Taggart, private papers.

21. Hayes, op. cit., p. 97.

22. Hurley, op.cit., pp. 84-5.

23. Ellis, op. cit., p. 110.

24. Hurley and Ellis, op. cit, p. 22.

25. Ibid., pp. 3-4.

26. J. Cooney, article in *Doctrine and Life,* September 1973, pp. 499-502.

27. Hurley and Ellis, op. cit., pp. 27-8 and 57.

CHAPTER 4: THE ICC: SUCCESSES, CRITICISMS AND CHALLENGES

1. Forty-eighth annual report, ICC, p. 6.

2. Taggart, private papers, address by Gallagher to ICC, 6 November.

3. Taggart, private papers, address by Taggart to ICC, 13 April 1972.

4. In *New Divinity* – described as 'a Church of Ireland journal, summer 1972 – vol. 3, no. 1, pp. 103-10.

5. Quoted in Hurley and Ellis, op. cit., pp. 37-8.

6. 'The unity that really matters', an article by me in the *Irish Christian Advocate*, 16 January 1969.

Bibliography

I: MINUTES OF THE ICC COUNCIL MEETINGS

Minutes of the ICC Executive Committee and ICC Council meetings
Annual Reports of the ICC
Minutes of the ICC/RC Joint Group meetings
Minutes of the Belfast Council of Churches (held at ICC)

II: PRIVATE PAPERS

Dr Gallagher's private papers for the period 1968-74 (held by Dr Dennis Cooke)
Taggart's private papers

III: BOOKS AND BOOKLETS

Barkley, John M., *The Irish Council of Churches 1923-1983*, Belfast 1983
Barkley, John M., *Blackmouth & Dissenter*, Belfast 1991
Bew, Paul and Gillespie, Gordon, *Northern Ireland: A Chronology of the Troubles 1968-1999*, Dublin 1993
Bleakley, David, *Peace in Ulster*, London 1972
Bloomfield, Ken, *Stormont in Crisis*, Belfast 1994
Boyd, Robin, *Ireland: Christianity discredited or pilgrim's progress?*, Geneva 1988
Cooke, Dennis, *Persecuting Zeal, A Portrait of Ian Paisley*, Dingle 1996
Cooney, John, *John Charles McQuaid, Ruler of Catholic Ireland*, Dublin 1999
Dunlop, John, *A Precarious Belonging, Presbyterians and the Conflict in Ireland*, Belfast 1995
Eames, Robin, *Chains to be Broken*, London 1992
Elliott, Sydney and Flackes, W. D., *Northern Ireland: A Political Directory 1968-1999*, Belfast 1999
Ellis, Ian, *Vision and Reality, A Survey of Twentieth Century Irish Inter-Church Relations*, Belfast 1992
Ellis, Ian and Hurley, Michael, *The Irish Inter-Church Meeting: Background and Development*, Belfast 1998
English, Richard, *Armed Struggle, A History of the IRA*, London 2003
Faulkner, Brian, *Memoirs of a Statesman*, London 1978
Fey, Harold E. (ed), *The Ecumenical Advance: A History of the Ecumenical Movement 1948-1968*, vol. 2, Geneva 1970

Gailey, Andrew, *Crying in the Wilderness, Jack Sayers 1939-69*, Belfast 1995

Gallagher, Eric and Worrall, Stanley, *Christians in Ulster 1968-1980*, Oxford 1982

Hayes, Maurice, *Minority Verdict: Experiences of a Catholic Public Servant*, Belfast 1995

Hurley, Michael, *Christian Unity: an ecumenical second spring?*, Dublin 1998

Hurley, Michael, *Healing and Hope: Memories of an Irish Ecumenist*, Blackrock 2003

Ledwith, Michael, and Gallagher, Eric, *Ecumenism in Ireland: Experiments and Achievements*, (no location) 1981

Mayne, Brian, *Changing Scenes*, Blackrock 2003

Megahey, Alan, *The Irish Protestant Churches in the Twentieth Century*, London 2000

McIvor, Basil, *Hope Deferred: Experiences of an Irish Unionist*, Belfast 1998

McKittrick, David; Kelters, Seamus; Feeney, Brian; and Thornton, Chris, *Lost Lives*, Edinburgh 1999

McKittrick, David, and McVea, David, *Making Sense of the Troubles*, Belfast 2000

Morrow, John, *On the Road of Reconciliation*, Blackrock 2003

O'Neill, Terence, *The Autobiography*, London 1972

Patterson, Carlisle, *Over the Hill: Ecumenism in the Presbyterian Church*, Belfast 1997

Rose, Peter, *How the Troubles Came to Northern Ireland*, Basingstoke 2001

Violence in Ireland: A Report to the Churches, Belfast 1976

Index

of selected people, places and themes